The CAREER Itch

4 STEPS for TAKING CONTROL of WHAT YOU DO NEXT

Grace Owen

o g
publishing

This book is dedicated to my father,
Thompson Benjamin Coleman
1933–2004

og publishing
A division of Grace Owen Solutions Ltd
PO Box 56791, London E11 9BP

A CIP catalogue record for this book is available from the British Library

ISBN 978-0-9563908-0-6

Editorial Team: Jacqueline Burns, Leda Sammarco and Jane Collinson
Design and illustration © Julia Lloyd   Photography by Jake Green
Printed in the UK by MPG Biddles Ltd

2 4 6 8 10 9 7 5 3 1

Mixed Sources
Product group from well-managed forests, controlled sources and recycled wood or fiber
www.fsc.org Cert no. TT-COC-002303
© 1996 Forest Stewardship Council
FSC

10% of proceeds from the sale of this book
will go to support AIDS orphans in Africa

CONTENTS

ACKNOWLEDGEMENTS

To my husband Simon, for his love, honesty and patience. To my son Ben for the news updates and hugs. To my sister Rev Dr Kate Coleman, for keeping me focused. To Rose Coleman, another sister, for IT support and childminding...where would I have found the time without you?! To Maame Coleman, yet another sister, and Rev Cham Kaur Mann for your constant encouragement and curiosity throughout the 'birthing' of this book.

Thanks to Sue and Brian Owen for their suggestions and excellent proofreading skills. To Victoria McMillan and Claire Ward for their time and 'fresh' pairs of eyes! Thanks to the Owen family for their ongoing interest.

To my support team (mum, Rev Alison Mackay, Becky Salmon-Craig, Emma Sawyerr, Fiona Beckford, Joyce Strong, Lynda Bickley, Pastor Sandra Thomas and Sara Kruger) for their enthusiasm, calls and emails.

Thanks to my past employers who gave me a story to tell. To my clients and fellow Career Itch-ers, who have shared the highs and lows of their career journey with me. To Kate Bradley at HarperCollins who first saw potential in this book and got my foot in the publishing door.

To Sue Blake for getting me started and the editorial team Jacqueline Burns, Leda Sammarco and Jane Collinson for their incredible patience in helping me to shape the finer details. To Roan Media and Moore VA for taking me into the 'big wide world'. To Julia Lloyd for her fabulous cover designs…I will have to write more books to use them all! Thanks to Biddles for a great print job and Duncan Beal at York Publishing Services for sharing your expertise and car!

To readers of *The Career Itch*, I have written this book to be a source of practical inspiration. May it be just what you are looking for…enjoy!

INTRODUCTION

"There are no rules you can follow, you have to go by instinct and be brave" Unknown

MY STORY...

It was Millennium Eve, a few minutes to midnight and I could feel the crowd getting more excited as they started to jostle and shout. I was on a rooftop at London Bridge waiting for the fireworks to start, when the inner restlessness about my career returned. What did this feeling mean? Was it something to do with having turned 30 the year before? Maybe it was the global excitement about entering a new century that was unsettling me? I couldn't put my finger on the growing ache but as Big Ben struck midnight, I vowed that I wouldn't feel like this on the eve of 2001.

I named the inner restlessness that I felt that evening *The Career Itch*. This was because it described the mixture of feelings that I had about my future career, including confusion, frustration, hope and curiosity. It led me down a path of self discovery that enabled me to take control of what I did next. *The Career Itch* is what led me ultimately to become a career coach, speaker and author.

My career has taken a variety of twists and turns. I started out on the Marks and Spencer graduate management trainee programme. After completing it successfully, I worked as a human resources (HR) practitioner in stores overseeing a wide range of areas from staffing to payroll and performance management to employee welfare. I moved to the Marks and Spencer head office in central London, having decided to specialise in Learning and Development, which is one of the many branches of HR. This branch closely reflected my growing passion for equipping people to excel at work, and was a natural progression into the field of career development and change, which is now my area of expertise.

Soon after my experience on Millennium Eve I resigned from Marks and Spencer to commence an eight-month career break and figure out what to do next. On the eve of 2001, the inner restlessness had subsided and I felt content. The following January I took a temporary job, as a senior HR project manager at Whitbread, which became permanent. A year later I was approached to head up the learning and development team at Costa Coffee.

When *The Career Itch* returned three years later, I resigned from Costa Coffee to retrain and expand my skills in coaching, which I had come to love. I started a business that same year working as a freelance trainer, coach and consultant. Since then I have grown a diverse portfolio of work that has taken me into the public, private, voluntary and charity sectors. Developing this career smorgasbord has been exciting, challenging and enlightening.

During my professional life, I've met hundreds of

people at different stages of their career. Few are contented; most are looking for a sense of purpose and direction. Others are planning their next move in order to do something meaningful or earn more money. I have had conversations with students, professionals and managers, leaders of teams and working mums, entrepreneurs, undergraduates, postgraduates and people nearing retirement. From the shop floor to the boardroom I have listened to their stories, recognised their dilemmas, celebrated their successes and empathised with their difficulties.

After hearing so many people struggle with *The Career Itch* I finally decided to write this book, and hope that it will guide you through your feelings and take you where you want to go.

Whether you consider your career a series of jobs or a vocation, *The Career Itch* is an inner wake-up call and a trigger to take control of what you do next. It draws your attention to something that is just around the corner or coming over the horizon of your working life. We will look at *The Career Itch* in more depth later on.

Having told you my story, I would like to find out more about what is happening in your career right now. I wonder what has led you to pick up this book and what has brought you to where you are today.

YOUR CAREER SITUATION

Take this short self assessment and circle one letter in each category that best represents what is going on for you currently.

How do you spend a typical workday?

a) Working all hours God sends

b) Doing just enough to get things done

c) I am not working right now

d) Thinking about what I'd like to do next

What best describes how you feel about your career?

a) Running on empty

b) Going through the motions

c) Out of the loop

d) Uncertain about my next move

What are your thoughts on a Monday morning?

a) I can't go on like this much longer

b) I feel stuck

c) I'd like to return to work of some kind

d) I'm ready to move on to something new

What are you most likely to do in the evenings?

a) More work

b) Forget about work and chill out

c) Deal with personal or family concerns

d) Surf the internet looking for jobs

5 How would you advise your best friends if they were in your position?

a) Tell them to take a holiday

b) Suggest that they focus on the positive aspects of their work

c) Find ways to boost their confidence

d) Encourage them to consider all their options

 6 What do you feel you need most right now?

a) Rest

b) Momentum

c) Perspective

d) Direction

 7 What do you want most from your career in the next 12 months?

a) To have improved my work-life balance

b) Feel that I have moved forward

c) The flexibility to juggle personal interests or family matters

d) A new opportunity or a bigger challenge in my present work

Interpreting your responses

There are four situations that are likely to reflect your career right now:

Mostly a = **Burnt out**

Mostly b = **In a rut**

Mostly c = **Taking a break**

Mostly d = **At a crossroads**

Have a look over the page to read more about your career situation and what you can do about it.

MOSTLY A
Burnt out

Situation You're stressed, feel trapped, overworked and are possibly underpaid. You lack energy and focus, and have lost sight of your career, which has 'come off the rails'. This is a crisis in waiting.

Cause You may be in denial about how you feel, having taken on too much work, or your work ethic has led you to believe that others expect you to drive yourself this hard.

Risk If you continue at this rate, you are going to have a breakdown (if you haven't already) and become unable to deliver what you are being paid to do.

Opportunity A crisis can also be a turning point that opens up a wealth of new possibilities. However, to explore what else is available to you, some things will have to change.

What to do It is possible that you are so used to this current style of working, that it feels normal. Slow down by reducing your hours a little at a time over the next month and by doing only what is absolutely essential. Learn to say no to more tasks, take a well-deserved weekend break or book some time off.

MOSTLY B
In a rut

Situation Your career has stagnated and your working life looks like a scene from the film *Groundhog Day*. The daily routine has taken its toll and the feeling of inertia leaves you feeling that you are unable to take any action.

Cause You have stayed too long in your current job or you keep ending up in the same type of work. This may be due to fear of the unknown or because doing something new feels like too much effort.

Risk It is likely that you have not reached the bottom of the groove that you're in. If it deepens, you'll become more lethargic and negative, while remaining powerless.

Opportunity It is possible to get out of the rut through willpower, effort and support. There is hope for you, if you are willing to take the action required.

What to do Accept you are stuck in a rut and quit blaming yourself or anyone else for it. Start to see the positive side of your work by making the most of the resources that are available to you e.g. get involved in a new project, take on more responsibility or develop new skills. Any one of these will bring about increased motivation if you are fully committed to making them happen.

MOSTLY C
Taking a break

Situation Things other than a career have been a priority in your life and you made a conscious choice not to progress your career, but now you are preparing to go back to work.

Cause Taking maternity or paternity leave, dealing with a health issue, looking after a relative, spending more time with family, coming to terms with being made redundant, travelling or doing voluntary work.

Risk Since you've been 'out of it' you may have lost confidence, or you may have enjoyed the break but are anxious about returning to a daily working routine.

Opportunity During the break you took stock of what is really important to you and are clear that flexibility between your personal and professional life is a must.

What to do Update your CV adding skills that have been developed or newly acquired. Contact a former colleague and invite them out for a coffee. This will bring you up to date with recent changes. You may have decided during your break that you want to work for yourself, if so this is something that you need to investigate further.

MOSTLY D
At a crossroads

Situation You don't feel challenged in your current role and have got itchy feet again. You believe the time has come to leave it behind and step out into the unknown, but you are not sure what path to take.

Cause You have achieved what you set out to do and are starting to get bored; work seems a little stale. You want a new challenge, something that will take you out of your comfort zone, perhaps into a new area altogether.

Risk Others may think you are disengaged from the job at hand or unable to commit for the long term. You could rush into another job without considering all your options.

Opportunity A fresh start will motivate you. When you start to investigate the range of possibilities open to you, this will increase your enthusiasm and have a positive effect on how you present yourself.

What to do Check your personal finances to ensure you have a nest egg to support you, if there is a period of unemployment. Think carefully about where you want to go next, and start to consider your options. Don't burn any bridges on departure because you might need to access past networks. Go out on a positive note.

I have experienced all four situations at different times during my career, as have many of my clients whether employed, unemployed or working in an independent capacity. These are not the only situations that reflect where you might have been or where you might end up in your career. However, in my experience I have found that *The Career Itch* most commonly affects people who find themselves in one of these four places. Remember not to judge your career situation whatever it may be. The important thing is to identify which one most closely describes where you are, and accept that this is where you are at today.

ASK FOR FEEDBACK

Now that you have identified your career situation, it is worth discussing it with other people. Choose between three and six people and ask their opinion.

They could be family, friends or colleagues. The important thing is that you trust them and that they are honest and objective in sharing their thoughts. Why? We all get blinkered and develop tunnel vision about our careers and where we think we are. You may not be seeing things exactly as they are, and in any case other people's insights and views can often give you greater perspective. Start asking!

THE CAREER LANDSCAPE

In the 21st century there is no longer a job for life. In the past, people accepted that they would probably do one thing all their lives (possibly at the same company) and then retire. We now have a world of possibilities. With the arrival of the dot com era, globalisation, outsourcing, around-the-clock working and economic uncertainty, the career landscape has taken on a new shape, shifting away from one job and towards multiple jobs. Today there are a range of possibilities for the 21st-century worker to consider.

Paying attention to *The Career Itch* and learning to manage your own career will help you to make the most of all the opportunities out there. What is on offer? You can be employed on a full-time, part-time, temporary, permanent, job share or project basis. You may even choose to work for someone during the week and run a side venture in the evenings and at weekends. Alternatively you may decide to go freelance, work as an interim contractor or run your own business. Fifty per cent of my clients have started out as employees before moving on to do their own thing and building a bespoke portfolio of work.

In 1982, Charles Handy first coined the phrase 'portfolio worker'. In his book *The Hungry Spirit: Beyond Capitalism – A Quest for Purpose in the Modern World* he describes how there would be a switch from lives organised for us to ones we create, resulting in job portfolios with 'a collection of clients, a jigsaw of work', each part providing a different income stream. What Handy foresaw has now come to pass.

Having a bespoke career, rather than a one size fits all, also requires a professional network.

The internet and social networking mean that it is easier than ever before to connect with a wide range of people in addition to those that you come across at more traditional events like conferences. The people you meet can help you on your career journey because word of mouth is now an essential part of doing business. Networking helps you to find out about new jobs, broadens your contacts and ensures you are up to speed with what is happening in your industry and specialist area, whether you are employed, self employed or both.

The rapid developments in technology mean work can be carried out virtually as well as in an office, which facilitates a more flexible working style for both employees and the self-employed. Furthermore, micro-enterprises with strong creative and social values are springing up and making a significant contribution to economic growth.

The 21st-century world of work may be full of opportunities, but having so many choices can be daunting, and fluctuating economic factors can present challenges. It is essential to be savvy and pay attention to trends and changes going on in the wider world so

THE CAREER
LANDSCAPE 1909

that you can be proactive in managing your own career as well as your personal brand.

These days brands are no longer for multinational companies only; everyone is now their own brand (even if they choose to be an employee). In her book *Walking Tall: Key Steps to Total Image Impact*, personal branding expert Lesley Everett demonstrates that by identifying and harnessing your personal brand, you can authentically stand out from the crowd. Your unique personality, values, talents and transferable skills are the unique selling points (USPs) and currency with which you can negotiate the future work you desire to fulfil your career aspirations. This is where your personal power and influence lies.

The world of work will continue to evolve, as it has done over the past 40 years. According to career theorists, the baby boomers, born in 1946-1964, have traditionally climbed the career ladder to run companies and are motivated by leaving a legacy. Generation X, born during the period of 1965-1979, are often key decision

THE CAREER LANDSCAPE 2009

makers in organisations but are leaving employment to go it alone for the sake of work-life balance. Generation Y, born between 1980 to 1989, are internet buffs who have followed career paths that enable them to multi-task whilst achieving an integrated lifestyle and making a difference in the world.

No matter how the landscape shifts over the next 40 years, paying attention to *The Career Itch* will keep you one step ahead and able to deal with any upheavals. Then you can develop a truly satisfying and diverse career, whether this is working for different companies, becoming your own boss or a combination of both. It will also help you to enjoy a more flexible lifestyle (these days gap years are for grown-ups too!).

GET READY

Now you know more about me, have assessed your own situation and are aware of the landscape that lies ahead, you may be feeling curious, excited, have regrets or even feel in despair. Remember though, that there is no right or wrong about your situation; you are where you are. Acknowledging and accepting this is essential if you are to take control of what you do next.

The Career Itch is a sign that the time has come for some further inner exploration followed by action. Now, I would like to tell you about *The Career Itch* in more detail.

"The real voyage of discovery consists not in seeking new landscapes but in having new eyes" Marcel Proust

THE CAREER ITCH

What is the **CAREER Itch?**

In a nutshell it is...
An INNER RESTLESSNESS about the DIRECTION of YOUR CAREER

The Career Itch is like an internal alarm clock that carries on ringing even if you hit the snooze button; it may bug you during your daily commute or when you are working. It is, however, a symptom and not the cause of how you are feeling about your work. *The Career Itch* will stimulate you to reflect on where you are on your career path, and act as a catalyst for what you do about it.

Here are five don'ts and dos to remember when *The Career Itch* shows up:

Don't

- Ignore it because you think something is wrong

- Suppress and deny it

- Think it will go away

- Be overwhelmed or afraid of it

- Try to get rid of it

Do

- Welcome it

- Acknowledge how you feel (at the very least to yourself)

- Get excited about it

- Share its arrival with a loved one

- Read this book from cover to cover!

My first experience of *The Career Itch* occurred after having worked for one employer for nearly eleven years. For the first six years my working life was safe and secure but during the seventh year it became suffocating and stale. I didn't realise what was happening and at first suppressed the inner restless desire rather than try to understand it. This was a very confusing and painful time in my life because I felt caught between a rock and a hard place.

The Career Itch may feel uncomfortable or even unwelcome, but treat it like a good friend who prompts you to face yourself. Responding to *The Career Itch* will increase your self-awareness and help you to become more authentic in your work.

Contrary to popular opinion having 'itchy feet' doesn't always herald a seismic change. Instead it signals an opportunity to enhance your career and increase your satisfaction. It may be a sideways move or more responsibility in your current role. Alternatively, you may opt for a big change such as going from employed to self-employed or deciding to become a specialist in a particular area.

Initially you may not know precisely what is on the horizon, but you need to pay attention to the intuitive nudges of *The Career Itch*. If you investigate where your feelings are coming from, you can proactively manage your career, rather than constantly finding yourself in the wrong job or aimlessly trying new things.

It is also an opportunity for personal growth as *The Career Itch* does challenge you to move out of your comfort zone and find greater meaning and purpose in what you do. If you pay attention to it throughout your life, then it will enable you to use your talents and skills to the full and make a contribution to those around you.

I have met a very small number of people who don't experience *The Career Itch*. Often they have known what they wanted to do from a very young age, and they have pursued it, staying open to any changes along the way. However, they are rare. Most people do experience *The Career Itch* many times in their lives. As I have stated, it is both necessary, beneficial and something to be embraced.

KEY SYMPTOMS OF THE CAREER ITCH

Here is a list of 30 concerns I have heard over many years of career coaching. These concerns are some symptoms of *The Career Itch*.

Tick all of those that apply to you.

○ *I want more out of my job*

○ *I'm a high achiever but am now making mistakes in areas of my work*

○ *I've outgrown my role and feel demotivated*

○ *I no longer feel stretched by what I do or committed to the work I do*

○ *I want to make a real difference every day*

○ *I am at the end of my professional career path and have nowhere to go*

○ *I love my work but know it is time to move on*

○ *I would take a redundancy package if it was offered to me*

○ *Learning new skills is important to me and I am not doing that*

⊗ *I want to do more with my life*

○ *My boss is moving on and I would like to do that job*

○ *I am struggling to keep up with the demands placed on me*

⊗ *My family and friends are fed up with my constant whingeing about work*

⊗ *I hate my job. It bores me*

⊗ *This is not what I was born to do*

◯ *I am at a career crossroads. Which way do I turn?*

◯ *I have achieved everything I set out to. What's next?*

⊗ *I frequently ask myself, is this it?*

◯ *I'm not fulfilling my potential*

◯ *I have hit a glass (or concrete) ceiling*

◯ *I feel as if 'forces' want me out*

◯ *I have just resigned*

⊗ *I feel troubled and frustrated but don't understand why*

◯ *I am underpaid and overworked*

◯ *I am paid well and still overworked*

◯ *The job isn't what was 'sold' to me at the interview*

◯ *I am a square peg in a round hole*

⊗ *I want to change career but don't know how*

◯ *I can't see the wood for the trees*

◯ *I am returning to work after a career break and am not sure what I want to do*

How many symptoms did you tick? . . . . 7 . . . .

(write the number here)

If you have ticked three or more career concerns you have definitely got *The Career Itch*, and the time has come to do some serious soul searching. Don't waste one more precious moment; start taking control today.

HOW ITCHY ARE YOU?

Use the itch-o-meter below to rate the intensity of your restlessness on a typical working day. Don't think too much about it or try to be too precise; just trust your gut instinct. What is important is to gain a general idea of how you are feeling. Mark your rating on the itch-o-meter by making a note on the diagram or elsewhere for future reference.

The itch-o-meter enables you to see clearly the extent of your feelings about your career, so that you can openly acknowledge them. What else are you feeling?

Remember that you will always get itchy. *The Career Itch* doesn't just kick in when you have fallen out of love with what you do day-to-day. It is a driving force of professional (and personal) transformation. It will help to keep your working life fresh and interesting,

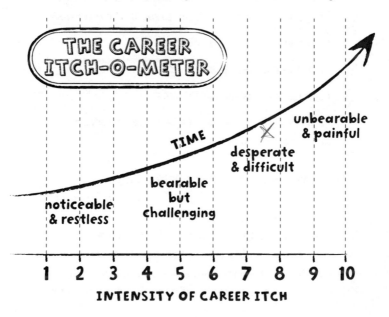

remind you when your work and other areas of your life are out of balance, and help you to develop a rich tapestry of knowledge, experience and skills. It can even move you closer to the legacy that you seek to leave behind, and draw you towards areas of work that enable you to make a difference.

Since Millennium Eve I have had four distinct career phases each one preceded by *The Career Itch*. Now I have learned to read the writing on the wall well before it is time to make the transition to something new. In my experience this occurs every two to three years! When *The Career Itch* returns, I listen and respond positively. We have become well acquainted, and it takes less time to work out what is happening to me although there are always surprises! Having diagnosed *The Career Itch*, I realised that it had wider implications, not just for me but also for others.

POTENTIAL BENEFITS FOR YOUR LIFE

Paying attention to *The Career Itch* has enabled me to choose work that is congruent with my values and beliefs. This has had a positive effect on other areas of my life and I now take better care of my health, ensure that I spend quality time with my husband and son, see family and friends regularly, and contribute to my local community.

Responding to *The Career Itch* can bring you so much more than money and perks. It can provide an opportunity for you to be true to yourself and when you are authentic in your work, it can have a positive effect in other areas of your life because they are all interconnected. This is a real work-life balance.

THE FOUR STEPS...

In this book I offer you practical steps, which are based on the acronym ITCH. Together these steps outline the 'big picture' of how to proactively manage your career. Each step is accompanied by things for you to do.

T is for **Thinking** = clarifying what you do next

2

I is for **Identity** = Knowing who you are

1

H is for **Habit** = achieving a balanced lifestyle

4

C is for **Change** = making a successful transition

3

Working through this book is like having a personal consultation with me. It is designed to bring you a fresh perspective on what you could do next to further your career. I will share real life examples of people I have worked with, to encourage and inspire you along the way.

Here are some tips to help you get the most out of this book:

- *Work through the steps in order allowing plenty of time to complete each one thoroughly, before moving on to the next. If you come across something that doesn't resonate with you, then keep an open mind. It may highlight an area of potential growth for you.*

- *Don't be tempted to skip the 'things for you to do' as they are an important part of the whole process. If you have trouble with any of them, take a break or discuss it with someone who knows you well and whose opinion you trust. Consider setting yourself a target of completing one step per week.*

- *Make notes as you go along. I write in all the self-help books I read because to me they are study guides. Alternatively, treat yourself to a gorgeous journal to record your ideas and insights.*

- *Read the book with a positive intention. This will help you to become aware of new opportunities and guide you in deciding what is best for you to do next.*

- **The Career Itch** *is about the journey as much as the destination. As I have explained it will appear at many stages of your career; it's not a one-off. You may discover your purpose in life through reading this book (and if so, that's wonderful), but you may simply find the next stage on your career journey and in the process get to know yourself better.*

YOU CAN TAKE CONTROL

When I first experienced *The Career Itch*, I felt powerless and alone. However, I believe that there are millions of other people experiencing *The Career Itch* at any one time; it is a universal human experience. Statistics show that in the UK 67% of people are dissatisfied with their job while 57% of people say that given their time again, they would choose a different career.

Since you are reading this book you probably don't feel in control of your career. However, you have a much greater degree of control than you have been led to believe. Taking control of what you do next will help you move towards inner peace and a sense of adventure, rather than fear or denial. It will open up a whole new world in which you can enjoy your career and develop your full potential.

The Serenity Prayer best sums this up:

> "God, grant me the serenity
> to accept the things
> I cannot change
>
> Courage to change the
> things I can and wisdom
> to know the difference"

Reinhold Niebuhr, Theologian

In the February after Millennium Eve, I went on a personal development course and on the first day had a major insight, namely that my career was like a blank canvas on which I could create the career of my dreams. Up till then my career had been dictated to me by family and careers advisors, to name a few! This insight enabled me to accept the things that I could not change such as the restructures and redundancies that were affecting my colleagues at that time. Instead, I summoned up the courage to resign, and during my eight-month career break spent quality time thinking about what I would do next, before taking further action.

In essence, the past ten years have taught me that when you focus on making something happen, it does. Becoming aware of your career situation is just the starting point. Courage is about taking small, deliberate steps to set you on your way. You have more control over the future of your career than you realise.

You are about to take a journey into the unknown and it may feel scary, but think about what you'll gain by responding to *The Career Itch* and what you'll lose if you don't. This process is like running a marathon rather than a sprint. If you have never run a marathon before it will test you; it takes time, preparation and stamina. It is a long-haul race but you will cross the finish line and in this race you are the only competitor. When you hit the wall of resistance, feel powerless or confused, try to relax. It is normal and it will pass!

START NOW

It is your choice whether to dip your toe into this experience or dive into the deep end! The more willing you are, the deeper you go and the greater your chances of a professional and personal transformation.

Each of the four steps is a milestone that marks your progress. Self-help can be lonely and difficult, so whatever you decide to do next, my role is to be your career coach. I will help you discover your own solutions and share some of mine. I want the best for you because you deserve to enjoy every moment of your career. I'll encourage and support you along the way.

Sign this personal declaration as a demonstration of your commitment to do what it takes to complete the journey with me. Doing this is an act of courage and one of many small steps.

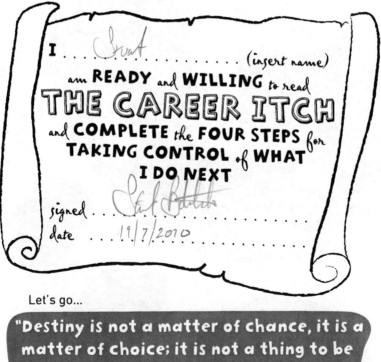

I .... *Grat* .... (*insert name*)
am **READY** and **WILLING** to read
THE CAREER ITCH
and **COMPLETE** the **FOUR STEPS** for
TAKING CONTROL of **WHAT**
I DO NEXT

signed ....
date 19/7/2010

Let's go...

"Destiny is not a matter of chance, it is a matter of choice; it is not a thing to be waited for, it is a thing to be achieved"

William Jennings Bryan

is for

IDENTITY

Knowing who you are

KNOW THYSELF

> "If you are not being yourself at work...who are you being?" Grace Owen

Who am I? Human beings have asked this question since the dawning of time. If you haven't asked this question at some point during your career, it is likely to crop up. Understanding who you are is a lifelong journey. When you experience *The Career Itch*, there are certain aspects of your identity that you need to consider, so that you can take control of what you do next in your working life.

You don't have to know the big picture around your career to map out the next stage but when you know who you are, at the current stage in your career, then you will be true to yourself, make the right choices, and your work will be more enjoyable. If you lack self-awareness you risk making unconscious career choices and wandering aimlessly from one job to the next.

Even in the 21st-century workplace the identity of many people is still bound up in their job title. This may be because they have been doing one thing for a very long time or because it gives them a sense of status. In fact, some people are so attached to their role that they can become a different person at work altogether.

Colin, a good friend of mine, told me that for years his father arrived home from work in a bad mood creating a tense atmosphere as soon as his foot crossed the threshold. When his father retired the whole family was invited to his leaving party. Colin was amazed at how many of his father's colleagues liked him. They said he was fun to work with; sadly this did not match Colin's experience at home. With hindsight, he believes that his father relished his senior role in the workplace and didn't feel this same enjoyment at home.

Putting on a mask or assuming a different persona can become stressful as you try to maintain multiple identities at work and home. I can understand this, as I became a corporate chameleon while progressing through the early part of my career. I was constantly chopping and changing who I was depending on the individuals or groups I interacted with. It has taken the past ten years for me to feel comfortable in my own skin and be true to myself. Doing this has made me far more effective at my job because I now have greater self-awareness and confidence.

Being real at work is a challenge but I believe that the more real you become, the more fulfilled you will be. It can be tempting to conceal aspects of yourself to fit in with the crowd and be liked, but in the long term this will make you very unhappy. When you are authentic you have more presence and people are more able to trust and respect you. You will also find that you draw the right people to you, whether they are colleagues, bosses or clients.

The real you goes way beyond the job title on your business card or email. Your title merely refers to what you do; it isn't who you are and *The Career Itch* is a reminder of this.

Remember that in today's workplace your identity also forms part of your personal brand, and like any brand you have unique selling points (or USPs) that set you apart from other people, even if you appear similar on the outside. These USPs are your personality, career values, talents and transferable skills. Expressing these aspects of your identity and being true to them will help to set you apart and get you noticed in the crowded marketplace.

My experiences of *The Career Itch* have shown me that understanding these elements will help you to create fresh opportunities, win new business, attract loyal team members, build a network of associates and be known in your field. As you confidently and sensitively express who you are, people who resonate with your personal brand and what it represents will engage with you, whether they are similar people or ones who complement you.

UNVEIL YOUR PERSONALITY

Your personality is complex and it is one of the things that clients and employers want to understand, because it reveals who you are. That knowledge will partly help someone to decide whether to hire you for a particular role or engage you for a project.

Over the past fifteen years I have come across many personality assessment tools. I have used these regularly in the work I do and they have really helped me to distinguish my character traits and understand where my strengths and weaknesses lie. I recall a colleague of mine who was a high achiever and driven to succeed, but this drive caused her to be brusque with people who weren't as driven as her. Understanding this strength and weakness helped her adapt to other people's personalities, whilst still getting the job done to the high standard that she desired.

I first became aware of how personality related to careers in an article in *The Sunday Times* magazine, which featured the work of Siobhan Hamilton-Philips, a well-known career psychologist. It explained that certain personality types had a preference for certain roles and industries. This interested me because I had not made that connection before. The client case studies further validated these assertions, which fuelled my curiosity because I had taken a raft of general personality assessments but not ones specifically linked to careers.

Rather fortuitously, I was doing some research into career development for senior managers at Costa Coffee and became a guinea pig on behalf of the business by signing up to a day's session with Siobhan herself! In the morning I completed several questionnaires related to my personality. These were processed into a report which she discussed in detail with me.

Discussing my personality in such depth gave me valuable insights into my relationships with people, my way of thinking and my feelings and emotions. For example, I discovered that I had a capacity for developing strategies and attracting new business, which was encouraging. The report also confirmed my interest in working with people, which was reassuring. In particular, finding out about these additional aspects of my personality gave me a confidence boost because I discovered just how well suited I was for my role as head of learning and development at Costa Coffee.

Overall, the career psychology experience helped me to take a more strategic approach to my work and find the best way forward through various issues. I spent more time developing stakeholder relationships and learning about external factors which were having an impact on the business, so that as a team we could respond more effectively. My preference for developing new business was useful to me when I set out on the path of self-employment and became responsible for finding and creating work.

Since then, I have returned to see Siobhan every few years because each report highlights the subtle changes in my personality as my career progresses. Through discussion, I determine how best to make use of these changes to continue with the work I do or create new opportunities.

THINGS for YOU to DO

ANSWER THE FOLLOWING QUESTIONS ABOUT YOUR PERSONALITY:

- How well do you know yourself?

- How would you describe your personality?

- What aspects of it are helpful in the work you do?

- What aspects of it are unhelpful in the work you do?

- What feedback do others give you about your personality?

- What types of people do you enjoy working with?

- What types of people do you find it difficult to work with?

- How has your personality changed as your career has progressed?

- What does the career situation that you are in (see page 10) tell you about your personality?

PERSONALITY PAYS OFF

At Costa Coffee a number of senior managers went along for the same independent assessment of their personality, interests and aptitudes. The feedback was unanimous. Not only did they find it beneficial to look more closely at their distinctive characteristics, but they used the information to improve their working relationships and determine the direction of their career.

DISCOVER YOUR CAREER VALUES

> "People work best when they are passionate about what they do"

Grace Owen

ARTI'S STORY

'What is important to you about your career?' Arti stared at me with a blank expression. I asked the question again, this time more slowly. Arti contacted me through a family friend and told me that she was feeling demotivated. On the itch-o-meter she rated herself as an 8 and wanted to investigate what was going on for her.

After eight years of being employed, she had decided to try freelancing as she wanted a more flexible lifestyle. She had been doing this for nearly five years when she first came to see me.

The first three years had been particularly tough because she didn't enjoy networking as it felt like 'selling' but she kept at it, had grown in confidence, and now had a number of core clients. Sales were steady

*and she was happy with the profit margin. This meant
that she could cover the cost of running the business
and pay herself a decent wage with a small sum left
over to develop ideas for passive income streams, so
that she could make money while she slept.*

*Arti finally replied, 'What do you mean by
important? I do what I need to get the job done.'*

Your career values are like guiding principles that
become more important to you as your career
progresses. I have the following eight career values
which are listed in order of importance.

Authenticity
Being true to who I am
and the work I do

Lifestyle
A portfolio of work that
enables me to have flexibility

Specialist
Focusing on doing a few
things very well

Contribution
Equipping people to excel
in their work

Relationships
Building mutually beneficial
alliances with others

Professionalism
Doing a great job,
consistently

Diversity
Working with people from
different industries

Expertise
Developing my professional
knowledge and skills

When I defined my career values for the first time,
I became fully aware as to why I had been feeling so
lethargic and disinterested at work. I realised that at the
time, my top four career values were not being satisfied
in the work I was doing. This knowledge brought such
relief that I cried! I started to understand why the inner
restlessness around my career was happening.

Your career values keep you motivated and engaged
at work. They help you to make the right decisions
about what is important in your job and your overall
career. At the start of a career you may be motivated
by basic financial security; most people are. However,
as you go along the desire for additional material
possessions may no longer satisfy you. Your career
values may shift from money to making a difference,
from working in a large organisation to working in a
small one, from being a generalist to being a specialist,
and so forth.

Career values are not the same as a work ethic,
which is something that is often culturally imposed
or absorbed like the Protestant work ethic. They
are traditions that we have grown up with and don't
question. For example, in my family I grew up with
an African work ethic demonstrated by my father.
He believed that education was essential for carving

out a meaningful career and that working every hour possible to provide for the family was his main purpose in life.

Career values are not the same as the organisation's values that have been developed as part of a marketing strategy or employer brand exercise. If you are working for yourself then your own values will make up your brand. Career values are yours and yours alone. They are those things that you are passionate about and hold true.

Your career values are a checklist for what you are looking to express and experience in your current project or next job. I use mine in this way when new opportunities arise, so that I can assess whether the offer of work is in line with my values, particularly the top four, which are the most important to me. You may not satisfy all your career values all the time, but it is still important that you know what they are and what they mean to you. Then you can revisit each career value, which may change over time, and find imaginative ways to realise it more fully.

To find your career values (or rediscover them) and use them to create the working life you seek, it is important to review them at least once a year because they change. The things that were important to you twelve months ago may not be radically different, but even slight changes can affect your drive and enthusiasm. Firstly, you must become aware of them.

Recognition Praise.
Sense of achievement -

advancement promotion.
Flexible Lifestyle -

Learning new skills,
Professional -
Free to express
myself.

Freedom

-Successful ££
in control of own destiny.

Working with
nice people

THINGS
for YOU to DO

Being part of the
real world...
Not office
bound.

ANSWER THE FOLLOWING QUESTIONS
ABOUT YOUR WORKING LIFE TO DATE:

• Enjoy working

- ○ **What do you value in a career?**

- ○ **What motivates you in your current work?**

Thought of being sacked

Nothing

- ○ **If you didn't need to earn a living, what**
  would you do? Write + take pictures + Travel!

- ○ **What do you love about your work?** I don't love my work
  These things energise and excite you

- ○ **What do you dislike about your work?** Lack of mgt.
  These things drain and bore you No team spirit.

People

Summarise what is important to you in your career by
writing a list of key words or phrases e.g. 'making a
difference' and a sentence or two about what that means
to you.

Once you have this list choose a maximum of eight that
are your top career values and prioritise them, putting the
most important first.

Consider how you can bring more of your career values
into your daily working life and ask yourself what you
would need to stop, start or continue to do, that would
make this happen.

Need to analyse situations

ARTI HAS A BREAKTHROUGH

With her career values defined, Arti was alarmed and pleased at the same time. Alarmed because she hadn't realised that her career values of freedom, creativity, teamwork and worth were so important to her, but pleased when she held these up against her freelancing work, as she immediately understood why she had been feeling stuck and demotivated. These values didn't feature to a great extent in her day-to-day work and, not surprisingly, The Career Itch *wake-up call was triggered.*

Most of Arti's time was spent on the phone to suppliers and trying to get through the constant emails. She felt handcuffed to her laptop. Arti missed being creative and meeting clients to discuss their changing needs. She spent a lot of time alone in her home office and was suffering from 'cabin fever'.

Understanding her career values was like a light bulb going on in her mind; she had clarity about her real passions for the first time. The Career Itch *had saved her from Groundhog Day!*

Arti now understood that each career value was directly linked to her level of motivation and inspiration on the job. Next she focused on finding new ways of fulfilling and honouring these career values in her freelancing business. Firstly, she prioritised her workload so that she could focus on the core aspects of her business which were building relationships with clients and generating new work. Secondly, she decided to look into hiring a virtual PA who could take on the administration. This would free up her time so she

could get out of her office more and start developing
ideas for the passive income streams.

STAY CONNECTED

When you know what your career values are and you stay
connected to them by putting them at the centre of what
you do, they bring purpose and focus to your daily work.

When you are disconnected from your career values
you are denying a fundamental part of who you are.
Your values are like an anchor, without which you will
be easily uprooted and displaced by the sometimes
unpredictable and stormy days of working life.

YOU'VE GOT TALENT

> "Hide not your talents. They for use were
> made. What's a sundial in the shade?"
>
> Benjamin Franklin

JANIS'S STORY

Janis had **The Career Itch** *and knew it. She had ticked
ten out of the thirty key symptoms, which confirmed
her assertions. She understood what her career
values (fun, structure, people and collaboration) meant
to her and had made sure that her current job allowed
her to express these each day, especially as she had
recently resigned from a job where she was unable
to do this. Now she loved her work and felt that she
was in an enviable situation compared to her friends,*

who complained about their jobs when they met for
drinks at the local pub on a Friday evening. She used
to complain once too.

However, Janis believed that she wasn't making the
best use of all her talents and wanted to know what
she could do to about this.

The modern world is obsessed with talent.
Traditionally it was used to describe people with
exceptional musical, sporting or academic ability. Now
it is a source of peak time television entertainment
(often with large amounts of money at stake!). However,
everyone has a talent (whether it is one or many);
they are God-given. You may have a flair for numbers,
words, cooking, sports, public speaking or working with
children. I read that Barack Obama has a particular
talent for motivating people who thought they were
powerless; clearly he put it to good use!

Just because you have a talent for something,
however, doesn't mean that you put it into practice. If
you switch around the l and the t in talent, you get the
word latent! Your talents can often lie dormant and
you may be completely unaware that you have any.
This is mainly because, when you are naturally good
at something, you can take it for granted, ignore it or
even believe it has no significance. You may not even
recognise your talents until someone else points them
out to you!

Knowing what your talents are is vital, particularly
when you are experiencing *The Career Itch*.

It will help you to do the best that you can, with what
you have and where you are right now.

THINGS
for YOU to DO

**COLLATE ANY INFORMATION THAT
PROVIDES EVIDENCE OF YOUR TALENTS**

Examples are: Pictures I have taken.

○ **Emails, cards or compliments from family
and friends about what you do well**

○ **Your recent appraisal or performance
review from work**

○ **Client testimonials and feedback that
confirm your natural strengths**

○ **Reports from personality or other
psychometric and behavioural tests**

○ **A university, college or school report –
these may remind you of things you have
forgotten about**

○ **Anything else that provides insights into
your talents e.g. certificates, an award or even
a feature in a local newspaper or magazine**

*Read through this information making a list of all your
talents (for example, humour, debating, explaining
things, painting, singing, cooking, making things,
planning, connecting with people etc) no matter how
small they may appear.* continued...

INTERVIEW THREE TO SIX PEOPLE, WHOM YOU TRUST AND WHO WILL BE FRANK WITH YOU

They could be family members, friends, work colleagues, your boss, a mentor or coach. Explain that you want them to help you to identify your talents by answering the following questions:

○ **What do you think I am naturally good at?**

○ **What is unique about me?**

○ **What do you value about me?** *Doing Man things. Practical Man skills. Promise family and care*

○ **Which three words best describe my talents?** *Calm, careful, creative*

○ **If my talents were a gift, what gift would they be?**

These interviews are designed to be fun. Ask that they provide you with clear and specific examples so that their comments are supported by factual information from real events (don't let them be vague, as it won't help you understand more about yourself). You might want to write down their responses, or ask them to do this (so that it is in their words and not yours).

Planning things (studs), Visualising problems, Foreseeing things. How people are going to want to do something. thinking steps ahead, foresight. Eloquent. Argument. Beating down problem at logical component. Attention to detail

continued...

Weighing up pro's and cons

Keeping an eye on bigger picture.

Calm exterior. Alert at night

USE YOUR TALENTS

The Career Itch will prompt you to unearth your talents and do something with them. You may use them to develop a niche or they may take you into many different areas. If you don't express your talents someone will be missing out on your divine gift!

JANIS DISCOVERS NEW TALENTS

When Janis had completed these actions we sat down together and analysed the results. Some of her talents had been unearthed years ago and were already in use. However, the big news for her, was that everyone she interviewed felt she was naturally good at communicating with clarity. This surprised her because at times she felt self-conscious when presenting to a group. Another talent that came to light was hospitality. Whenever clients arrived she was the first to welcome them, offer them refreshments and

show them around the facilities, whilst introducing
them to other members of staff. She loved meeting
and greeting new people.

This knowledge was a boost to Janis's self-esteem, giving her the reassurance to demonstrate these 'new' talents. When opportunities arose at work for speaking engagements she volunteered and over time increased her confidence. She was given additional responsibility for client hosting, which not only fulfilled her 'people' career value but was a great addition to her CV.

TALENT WILL OUT

I believe that every human being is naturally good at something (whether it is one thing or many). It is essential to discover and nurture your talents, so that you can share them with others. If you think about all the things you enjoy in life, such as food, clothes, your home, health, films, music and books, you realise that someone has used their talent to bring these gifts to you.

From your schooldays onwards you may have been told to focus on your weaknesses and make improvements in those areas that you were not so good at. However, you don't have to improve on your talents as they are innate; instead you can develop and explore them. Whilst other people may have similar talents, your life experience, personality and attitude give your talents a twist that is as individual as your fingerprint. Using your talents at work gives you satisfaction and makes you feel fulfilled. Along with your career values, they make you feel in tune with your true self.

You may still be feeling uncertain about what your talents are or even if you have any, but they will surface in the end, even if you have been diverted from your true path. When the time is right, they will appear.

As a child I enjoyed being creative. I loved to read, won a poetry competition, danced during school productions, sang in the school choir and played the classical guitar proficiently. However, my father, being a traditional African man, wasn't keen that I make a career out of being creative because he believed that I wouldn't earn a good living from it. When I was still young he channelled me in the direction of maths, biology, chemistry and physics rather than focusing on further developing my creative abilities. He was hoping that I would have a secure income for life by becoming a doctor or a scientist.

I didn't! After struggling for five years to do well in the sciences, I managed to succeed at biology, which wasn't top of his list and at university, signed up to do a joint degree in Biology and Dance studies (without his knowledge and to his displeasure. He got over it... eventually!). To this day people make jokes about me being a 'dancing biologist'!

Although I didn't follow a career path that took me into the arts or the scientific or medical field, I did learn how to think both creatively and logically, which has stood me in good stead throughout my career. In the end I found an opportunity to express my talents.

IDENTIFY YOUR
TRANSFERABLE SKILLS

"Employers rate 'transferable and flexible skills' as more important than traditional qualifications" Online poll by the Chartered Institute of Personnel and Development, 2009

MAURICE'S STORY

Maurice contacted me via my website. His email explained how he had been trying to update his CV for over six months but felt that it wasn't 'quite right'. He had heard about terms like transferable skills but was convinced that as a senior computer programmer, he only possessed technical skills.

Maurice wasn't planning to change jobs anytime soon but wanted to keep his options open. He had promised himself that he would keep his CV up to date as part of a New Year's resolution so that when The Career Itch did show up, he was ready to take control of what to do next.

A skill is typically something that you learn to do well and develop over time and may have its roots in your talents. Now that you have identified your talents, you may see a pattern emerging in terms of the type of skills you have acquired. There could be a common theme.

The level of your talent will be indicated by how skilful you become at something.

For example, you may be a dab hand at cooking and your family and friends may love having you cook for them. Becoming highly competent or a master chef like Madhur Jaffrey or Jamie Oliver takes your talent to another level. It involves years of practice and support from loved ones to become that accomplished. Talent is the raw material that must be carefully nurtured to deliver success. To be highly skilled at something calls for absolute focus, dedication and access to resources, be they time, money, people, information or opportunities.

We tend to think about transferable skills in the context of careers and the workplace. However, some of these skills may have been learned socially or in a voluntary capacity. Whatever their origins, they are portable and move with you throughout your career. They can be applied to both new and familiar situations.

For example, training skills can be used everywhere but may be referred to as teaching, mentoring or instructing. The essence of this skill is enabling people to work better. Another example is that of organising and planning skills, which may appear to be more directly related to project management. However, organising and planning are needed for everyday working life, whether it is simply getting to work on time, arranging a visit or conducting a meeting.

CORE SKILLS

You could potentially have hundreds of transferable skills but here are five skills categories that are typically important in the context of your career. They are:

 People
Communication
and leadership

 Creative
Problem solving
and innovation

 Technical
Programming and
construction

 Information
Research, analysis
and record keeping

 Presence
Poise and
rapport

If you think about the tasks that you carry out during a typical working week or during your spare time (e.g. a hobby or voluntary work) you may be surprised at just how many transferable skills you have. Your level of expertise will depend on how often you use a particular skill and this will be of particular interest to prospective employers and clients. In addition, keeping abreast of what the marketplace is looking for will help you to keep your skills up to date and develop new ones.

THINGS *for* YOU *to* DO

COMPLETE THE FOLLOWING TRANSFERABLE SKILLS AUDIT TO HELP YOU FIND OUT WHICH ONES YOU HAVE ALREADY ACQUIRED VERSUS THOSE THAT YOU MAY NEED FOR THE FUTURE

In the tables below are the five categories of the most common transferable skills.

Evaluating your level of effectiveness and enjoyment can boost your credibility and self-esteem when applying for jobs or meeting potential clients to win new business. Rate your effectiveness and your enjoyment level on a scale of 1 to 4, where:

4 = Highly Effective   Others see you as an expert and you love doing this

3 = Effective   You are confident in your ability and like to do this

2 = Being Developed   You are improving all the time, but it can still feel a bit awkward

1 = Ineffective   You are aware that you still have a lot to learn and struggle to do this

continued...

PEOPLE	EFFECTIVENESS	ENJOYMENT
Listening attentively	3	2
Training, teaching and developing people	2	2
Recognising achievements	2	2
Providing useful and timely feedback	~~3~~ 2	~~2~~ 1
Supporting others through change	~~2~~ 1	~~2~~ 1
Creating a vision and setting direction	3	~~3~~ 2
Influencing stakeholders positively	~~2~~ 1	2
Delegating respectfully	~~3~~ 2	~~3~~ 2
Showing empathy and awareness of others	~~3~~ 2	~~3~~ 2
Developing trust	3	2
Total score out of 40	21	17

CREATIVE	EFFECTIVENESS	ENJOYMENT
Using your intuition	3	3
Coming up with original ideas	3	3
Implementing solutions	2	2
Seeing patterns and connections	3	3
Looking at alternative ways of doing things	3	3
Embracing change readily	2	1
Making complex information simple	3	2
Lateral thinking	3	3
Seeing the big picture	3	3
Designing and developing	3	3
Total score out of 40	28	26

continued...

	EFFECTIVENESS	ENJOYMENT
TECHNICAL	3	3
Using a range of tools	3	4
Being good with your hands	3	2
Understanding systems	3	2
Customer/colleague support	3	3
Paying attention to detail	3	2
Developing programmes	3	3
Repairing equipment	4	4
An interest in electronic gadgets	2	2
Information Technology skills	1	1
Procurement management		
Total score out of 40	28	26
INFORMATION	3	2
Dealing with figures	3	2
Detail orientated	3	2
Logical thinking	3	2
Evaluating processes	3	2
Analysing information	3	3
Forecasting and monitoring	3	2
Gathering and extracting	3	2
Ensuring accuracy	3	1
Report writing	3	1
Indexing and archiving		
Total score out of 40	30	19

continued...

PRESENCE

	EFFECTIVENESS	ENJOYMENT
Self assurance	1	3
Able to engage and inspire	2	3
Driven and focused	2	4
Using self disclosure appropriately	1	1
Calm and composed	1	4
Authenticity	2	3
Able to challenge constructively	2	3
Establishing healthy boundaries	2	3
Feeling in control	1	4
Self awareness	2	3
Total score out of 40	16	31

- **Which areas had the highest scores for effectiveness?** INFORMATION
- **Which transferable skills do you most enjoy using?** PRESENCE
- **Which areas had the lowest scores? These indicate which of your skills may need to be improved. Always check if you enjoy them and if they are relevant to the work you do before investing time and resources.**

GET A SECOND OPINION

It is worthwhile sharing your results and answers with someone else. This will help you to develop a greater understanding of your transferable skills and enable you to communicate them more clearly to clients or employers.

MAURICE SHAPES UP HIS CV

Maurice completed the transferable skills audit and was amazed at just how many skills he had acquired during his career. In addition to his technical ability, he had strengths in the people and information categories in particular.

He made the various adjustments to his CV and I cast my eye over it to double check that it sounded and looked great. A few months afterwards, Maurice started to experience The Career Itch and used his CV to apply for a number of jobs. Whilst he hasn't had success yet, feedback about his CV was very positive and he has had several interviews. Since meeting with me, he has developed a ritual of updating his CV regularly to keep it fresh.

MAKE THE MOST OF YOUR IDENTITY

Your personality, career values, talents and transferable skills are the unique selling points of your identity. Though your personality and values may shift and the frequency and situations in which you use your talents and skills may fluctuate, they are a fundamental part of who you are. When *The Career Itch* strikes, it is definitely time to review them, but it is also worth doing this regularly with regards to your work, so you can ensure they remain an authentic part of your personal brand.

THE IMPORTANCE OF SELF-DEVELOPMENT

"One who learns, teaches" Ethiopian proverb

I am often asked by clients who have *The Career Itch*, 'how can I fulfil my potential at work?' Well, your potential is part of your identity and now that you have completed the previous exercises, you will be able to continue developing your personality, values, talents and transferable skills. In the section 'Know thyself', I mentioned that understanding who you are is a lifelong journey, and once you are committed to this, you are well on your way.

Self-development is how you fulfil your potential, learn about yourself and accept who you are, warts and all! I believe it is a key transferable skill that needs to be learned, whether you are self-employed or an employee. Why? When *The Career Itch* appears you can quickly work out which element of your identity has changed in relation to your career, so that you can determine how to move forward. Self-development is also the way to enhance your personal brand and over time will give you greater clarity when making decisions about your career path.

It does not mean that you will never make mistakes or fail. Someone once told me that to FAIL is to take the First Action In Learning, which I really like! As you take control of what you do next in your career, both success and failure mean that you're better equipped to do things differently the next time.

If you are an employee it is likely that you will be offered training opportunities. If so, do make the most of these because this will develop you personally and professionally. As a freelancer you may have to be more selective and cost-effective about your self-development, which may include attending courses or hiring a business coach. This is one way you can add further value to your clients; it will also increase your bottom line.

STEPH'S STORY

Already self-aware, Steph was coming to terms with her personality strengths and weaknesses. Over the past couple of years she had taken the time to discover her career values, talents and transferable skills.

Steph loved to learn and at times referred to herself as a 'learning addict'. She took every opportunity to develop because she believed that there was still untapped potential within her. Life, to her, was a learning experience and this was the attitude that had helped her to become so successful in her work in the healthcare profession, where she worked on a fixed contract basis.

Now Steph had decided that she wanted to take full responsibility for her self-development and determine how to bridge any gaps in her knowledge and skills, but she was struggling as to the best way of going about this.

With my help she was ready to take her self-knowledge and use it to move on to the next level in her career.

KEEPING IT SIMPLE

"Tell me and I'll forget, show me and I'll remember. Involve me and I'll understand" Confucius

Steph and I designed a bespoke self-development assessment, so that she could understand what stage she was at. This is what we came up with:

SELF-DEVELOPMENT	EFFECTIVENESS	PRIORITY	TIMESCALE
Utilising personality strengths	4	1	
Managing personality weaknesses	2	4	3 months
Reviewing career values	3	1	
Satisfying career values	4	1	
Expressing talents	4	1	
Eliciting hidden talents	3	1	
Updating professional skills	3	1	
Enhancing interpersonal skills	3	3	6 months
Creating opportunities for learning	1	1	9 months
Taking up opportunities for learning	3	2	

Total score out of 40   **30**

Steph assessed her effectiveness on a scale of 1 to 4, where:

4 = Highly Effective   **Others see you as an expert**
3 = Effective   **You are confident in your ability**
2 = Being Developed   **You are improving all the time**
1 = Ineffective   **You are aware that you still have a lot to learn**

Steph assessed her priority level on a scale of 1 to 4, where:

4 = **Urgent**   **Address in 3 months**
3 = **High Importance** **Address in 6 months**
2 = **Important**   **Address in 9 months**
1 = **Not Urgent**   **Address in 12 months**

Out of the ten self-development areas, she homed in on three. We then discussed how she would set goals and monitor her progress in these over the next nine months.

START A SELF-DEVELOPMENT PORTFOLIO

A self-development portfolio is an excellent way of logging and collating information about your learning experiences as you come to terms with *The Career Itch*. I recommend that you have four sections to your portfolio: personality, career values, talents and transferable skills. You may already have lots of ideas about what you aspire to in each of these areas, but this portfolio is the hard evidence of what you have done to cultivate yourself.

It is also important to remember that we all have different learning preferences. For example, it may be on your own, in a group, face to face or online, by reading, by doing and so on. In the 1970s Peter Honey and Alan Mumford developed a learning styles system, which is still relevant today. The four styles they identified are activists, reflectors, theorists and pragmatists. Knowing your style will accelerate your learning and you can find out which one you are by completing their learning styles questionnaire, which also includes a wide range of methods that best suit your style. (See 'Must-have resources' at the back of this book for more details on this.)

My learning style preference is a combination of sitting back to reflect and being hands-on and action-orientated. During my eight month sabbatical I did lots of self-development by thinking and journaling, reading books, listening to CDs and networking. I spoke with people I considered to be role models for advice and support. I requested feedback about my identity from family and friends and went to conferences, seminars and courses, both in the UK and in Europe. I hired a coach and found a mentor too. I also embarked on some voluntary work in a secondary school working with young adults. All of these activities were my efforts to develop new knowledge, understand myself and grow in self assurance.

WHAT IS IN A SELF-DEVELOPMENT PORTFOLIO?

The types of things that I have in my self-development portfolio are a range of:

- **Personality assessment reports**
- **An inventory of my career values**
- **Questionnaires to discover my talents**
- **Transferable skills audits**
- **A career plan**

I have used the results from these to provide information for the following:

- **CV**
- **Interviews**
- **Covering letters and emails**
- **Panel presentations**
- **Job application forms**
- **Freelancing (for proposals)**
- **Business opportunities (for tenders)**

Over the years I have added other things to my portfolio such as certificates of achievement, book reviews, course outlines and notes, newspaper or magazine interviews and diary entries. I now have a section dedicated to future self-development, which contains information about events, training programmes, books and assessment tools that can deepen the areas of my expertise and open up avenues for different types of work.

STEPH'S ANNUAL SELF-DEVELOPMENT REVIEW

Steph was thrilled to have a clear process and ideas for assessing and managing her self-development each year. By doing this she was able to wean herself off the need to take up every opportunity for learning and only choose those that would equip her to excel in her work and fulfil her potential. The greatest benefit of all was that by being more selective she had more time for leisure activities and to generate additional income.

THINGS for YOU to DO

- Complete Steph's self-development assessment

- Make a list of all the things you can put in your self-development portfolio

- Find out what is your preferred learning style

- Decide when you want to start a portfolio and get cracking!

- Create a personal profile to stay on track with each area of your identity; I have included mine as an example

GRACE OWEN
PERSONAL PROFILE

PERSONALITY

Reasonably independent and is prepared to go her own way rather than follow the group consensus. No strong need for the company of others, but likes regular contact with people. Grace likes to consult others before making a decision and is inclined to be critical of information and plans. A strong analytical theme extends to people, their motivations and behaviours. Intellectually curious, she prefers variety and novelty over routine and repetition in her work. She is totally dedicated to a task and brings energy to all she does.

Consistent feedback is that Grace has a warm, engaging and authentic style.

CAREER VALUES

- **Authenticity**   Being true to who I am and the work I do
- **Lifestyle**   A portfolio of work that enables me to have flexibility
- **Specialist**   Focusing on doing a few things very well

continued...

- **Contribution**   Equipping people to excel in their work
- **Relationships**   Building mutually beneficial alliances with others
- **Professionalism**   Doing a great job, consistently
- **Diversity**   Working with people from different industries
- **Expertise**   Developing my professional knowledge and skills

TALENTS

- **Strategic planning**   Goal orientated
- **Career coaching**   Naturally intuitive
- **Facilitation**   Enabling people to develop effective interpersonal skills
- **Communication**   Writing, speaking
- **Training**   Research, design and delivery of learning solutions

TRANSFERABLE SKILLS

- **Presence**   Poise and rapport
- **People**   Communication and leadership
- **Creative**   Problem solving and innovation

KEY CAREER ACHIEVEMENTS

Grace Owen is a career coach, speaker and author. She is an accredited coach, has an MSc in Learning and Development (with distinction) and a certificate in Entrepreneurship.

continued...

Over fifteen years she has equipped hundreds of middle to senior managers and professionals to manage and change their careers successfully. This work has taken her into leading organisations like London Business School, the BBC, Environment Agency, Brit Insurance, the NHS, Barclays Bank, Camden Council, the Crown Prosecution Service, Marks and Spencer, Whitbread and Costa Coffee. Grace has also equipped many people to make a successful transition from employment to going freelance or running their own business.

She has a reputation for bringing focus and clarity, generating direction and tangible results. Her first book, *The Career Itch*, was self-published.

Grace has been featured in the national press, online and in print. She was a guest speaker on radio, and in 2009 was one of the UK's leading career specialists in the One Life Live Career Clinic.

OTHER

Grace is passionate about voluntary work; she is a mentor to emerging leaders across a range of sectors and was involved in two innovative social enterprise charities. She was chair of a Youth Café management committee in North East London and held responsibility for the UK communications of a village regeneration project in Ghana, West Africa.

A personal profile can be adapted for many things including:

- **CV**
- **'About page' on a website**
- **Freelancing (for proposals)**
- **Social networking profiles**
- **Professional membership directories**
- **Business opportunities (for tenders)**

The fact that you are experiencing *The Career Itch* could mean that you are not making the most of your personality, using the talents or the skills that you most enjoy, or that your values are not in alignment with your work (or all four!). However, if you think back to a time when you weren't feeling 'itchy', then a completely different sensation should come to mind.

Now we have completed I is for Identity, Knowing Who You Are – the first of the four steps for taking control of what you do next – we move on to Thinking. All your hard work so far has laid a firm foundation for taking step number two!

"Nature never repeats herself, and the possibilities of one human soul will never be found in another"

Elizabeth Cady Stanton

is for

THINKING

Clarifying what you do next

PAUSE FOR THOUGHT

"Confusion comes before clarity"

Grace Owen

Now that you have considered who you are, and evaluated what you have to offer, it is time to go to the next level by revisiting your career situation and considering your beliefs, needs, aspirations and options.

You may feel that you have done enough thinking and are ready to move forward, but it isn't time to start updating your CV or looking for the next opportunity just yet. Alternatively, you may still feel confused about what to do next and if so, don't despair. This is a natural and healthy part of the process.

Experiencing *The Career Itch* will help you to become crystal clear about what you want to do next and although there may be hurdles along the way, you will make the transition. The important thing to remember is that you do have control over your thoughts about work.

It took a weekend personal development programme to make me aware of this! Up till then I had let others do the thinking about my career, allowing myself to be guided by my father, career advisors, line managers and the organisation where I had worked for eleven years.

During that weekend I started thinking about my career more deeply than I had ever done before. I did so much thinking that my brain ached, but by the end of three intensive days, I was ready to take action. *The Career Itch* was the catalyst that led me to contemplate my career; this has brought me to where I am today.

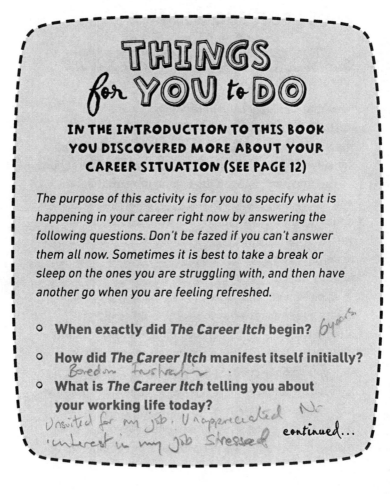

THINGS *for* YOU *to* DO

IN THE INTRODUCTION TO THIS BOOK YOU DISCOVERED MORE ABOUT YOUR CAREER SITUATION (SEE PAGE 12)

The purpose of this activity is for you to specify what is happening in your career right now by answering the following questions. Don't be fazed if you can't answer them all now. Sometimes it is best to take a break or sleep on the ones you are struggling with, and then have another go when you are feeling refreshed.

- When exactly did *The Career Itch* begin? 6 years.

- How did *The Career Itch* manifest itself initially? Boredom frustration.

- What is *The Career Itch* telling you about your working life today? Unsuited for my job. Unappreciated No interest in my job stressed

continued...

○ **What actions (if any) have you already taken to scratch *The Career Itch*?**

Re-read your responses to the key questions and add anything else that occurs to you. Then write a short statement that sums up what The Career Itch is telling you about your career situation.

Here is an example based on the experience I had that Millennium Eve:

> **My Career Itch *intensity rating is* eight (insert your own itch-o-meter rating from page 24) and I feel frustrated, confused and excited. The Career Itch *started in* 1999 and was sparked by a combination of things. *These were:* turning 30 years old, having worked for one company for almost eleven years, and seeing colleagues devastated by redundancy because they had invested so much of themselves in their role and the company. The Career Itch *is showing me that* the time has come to explore my options outside of Marks and Spencer.**

Thinking about the questions deeply will enable you to pinpoint precisely what The Career Itch is bringing to light. This is very important because often you can get emotionally caught up in the situation and are unable to see the wood for the trees.

It is also useful to share your statement with someone who knows you well and can challenge you on it if need be. You may need to rewrite the statement until it feels true for you.

THE ORIGIN OF BELIEFS

Your career has been directly and indirectly influenced by parents, teachers, colleagues and bosses. You will have inherited beliefs from them about what a career should be and have developed your own beliefs based on good and bad experiences. These are like an internal lens through which you perceive your current situation and make decisions about where to go in the future.

When beliefs are formed they go to one of two places. The first is the conscious mind, which is the part of us that is aware of what is going on now, what has happened in the past, and what it thinks may happen in the future. The second is the subconscious mind, which doesn't discriminate, but absorbs all beliefs without judgement, collecting lots of evidence from your daily working life to support them. Naturally you accept these beliefs as being true. From a young age into adolescence and adulthood, people and situations activate our beliefs.

THE IMPACT OF LIMITING BELIEFS

"One would accomplish many more things if we did not think of them as impossible" Malesherbes

CHARLOTTE'S STORY

Charlotte and I met on holiday. She explained that her career had come to a standstill after one year in a part-time job. She was also working in a local theatre for two nights a week, which she loved because it fulfilled her interest in amateur dramatics. She recognised The Career Itch *but didn't understand how or why it had appeared.*

As she talked about her day job the words she used to describe it were mostly negative. She complained of being overworked and said she felt stressed. I noticed that the tone of her voice was flat and her pace slow as she processed her thoughts into words. During our conversation, her head drooped, eye contact was minimal and she sat hunched over the table. Charlotte's whole demeanour was that of lethargy and resignation.

When I repeated back to her what I had heard, she sat up looking surprised and asked, 'Is that what I really said?'

Charlotte didn't realise that limiting beliefs were holding her back. These often result in self-sabotaging behaviour, fear or procrastination. Beliefs such as 'I can't do what I want', 'I don't deserve to have a great career' or 'I can't enjoy my working life' are obstacles that stop you responding positively to *The Career Itch*. You may be unaware of your limiting beliefs or hold onto them even when they are not serving you, because it feels less threatening to stay where you are than take a new step forward. Looking back I held on to my beliefs partly because it meant I could avoid taking responsibility for my career.

Empowering beliefs, on the other hand, move you towards the future that you truly desire. They can act as inner cheerleaders encouraging you to keep going even when things get tough. It is not simply a case of adopting a positive mental attitude; instead it is about developing an underlying belief system that supports you and is in tune with your personality, career values, talents and transferable skills.

If your empowering belief says 'I can do something', 'I will try anything once' or 'I am going to give this a go', you'll feel energised and will take action. Because you believe it is possible and you are willing to take calculated risks, the results you achieve will be more meaningful and bring you a greater sense of fulfilment.

SHIFTING LIMITING BELIEFS

Over the next few months Charlotte worked hard to shift old patterns of thinking to new ones, sometimes taking two steps forward and four steps back. During the first of our six coaching sessions she talked me through her career situation in more detail. As I asked questions, listened and reflected back what I heard, it soon became apparent that there were people and specific situations that made her feel particularly uncomfortable. As we examined these closely, Charlotte started to identify the limiting beliefs that she held in relation to them.

For instance, she believed that someone at work didn't like her and this belief was supported by the fact that she would dismiss Charlotte's opinions at client meetings and interrupt her in mid-sentence. Charlotte interpreted her colleague's behaviour as a vendetta against her and it was slowly eroding her self-esteem and confidence.

Charlotte hated team meetings because she felt that they were a waste of time and was unable to cope with the power plays and politics that went on. She spent most of the meeting in silent turmoil hoping for an opportunity to contribute which rarely came. As a result she would avoid making eye contact, speak only when spoken to and leave the meeting quickly, whilst others hung around for informal discussions. Her underlying belief was 'I lack authority', and as each weekly meeting approached, she tried to find ways of avoiding them, either by getting to work late or even calling in sick.

In my experience, the most effective way to deal with limiting beliefs is to start by:

- **Acknowledging that they exist. There is no point in pretending that they are not there, when they are clearly having a detrimental effect on your career**
- **Recognise that limiting beliefs are mental tracks that have been laid down in your mind over many years; it is unlikely that they will ever be erased completely**

- **Know that it is possible to create alternative mental pathways based on empowering beliefs, which can become your response of choice**
- **Be kind to yourself because you are learning to do something new. If you keep going you will start to see the benefits and this will motivate you even more**
- **Be patient, because over time your mental habits will automatically focus on what empowers rather than what limits you and your behaviour will authentically reflect this**

When you have a belief system that is empowering this will boost your self-belief. You will then find it easier to consider your work and career situation objectively and develop clarity about the changes you want to make.

CHARLOTTE TAKES ACTION

During our sessions, Charlotte imagined what it might be like to be in her colleagues' shoes or to be a 'fly on the wall'. This helped her to see things from a wider perspective and become more empathetic towards them. When I asked what stopped her from challenging her colleague's behaviour, she admitted that she simply didn't know how to go about it. She was afraid of drawing attention to the issues. The limiting beliefs that she held got in the way, so she didn't take action. Instead, she created two empowering beliefs. The first was 'I have something worthwhile to say' and the second, 'I do have authority'. She was determined to focus on these whenever old thinking patterns reappeared.

By session three of her coaching programme Charlotte had tried out a number of behavioural tactics to deal with the angst that had been created during the year. Firstly, she took her colleague to one side after a client meeting and asked what had led them to dismiss her opinion and interrupt her. To her surprise her colleague wasn't even aware of doing this, admitted that she often spoke without thinking, and apologised. Charlotte found that the best way of dealing with this was to let her talk, until she 'ran out of steam', before offering her own thoughts to the client. The biggest surprise for Charlotte was that, after the chat, her colleague eagerly invited her to make comments.

Secondly, she emailed her line manager about some of the issues she was experiencing in the team meetings and suggested solutions, such as having a clear agenda with timings for each item. She also suggested a rotating chair so that each member of the team could experience what it was like to manage their colleagues. In the meetings themselves she consciously changed her behaviour by speaking up to summarise a debate (which demonstrated her excellent listening skills), asking a 'naïve' question (which, she was soon admired for), and sharing her opinions (which were always well thought through). In addition to this, she spoke clearly and calmly, not rushing her comments, and she made eye contact whether listening or speaking. Over time, she too stayed around at the end of the meeting and started to build positive relationships with her boss and other members of her team.

In just a few months the dynamic of the team meetings changed. People were more considerate, said what needed to be said, and often dealt with individual issues before or after the meetings so that they didn't drag on through trying to resolve them. Charlotte's boss confided in her that the suggestions she had made were so helpful that they wished they had come up with them! Charlotte's strategy of empowering beliefs and matching behaviour was working!

SHIFT HAPPENS!

During our telephone sessions, Charlotte told me that her bosses and colleagues were so much more receptive to her and she began to like them and enjoy the day job. As we continued to discuss the changes that were taking place, it soon became clear to Charlotte that people were behaving differently towards her, because she was behaving that way towards them. They hadn't changed, she had. Charlotte's limiting beliefs reappeared from time to time, particularly in new situations, but she made the effort to adopt empowering beliefs and change her behaviour. As a result, she found that the limiting beliefs had less of a negative impact.

At session six of the coaching programme, we reviewed what was different for Charlotte. She said that the biggest insight she had was realising her limiting beliefs were not entirely true. As she started to question and put them to the test she realised that even if they felt 'true', avoiding certain people or situations wouldn't make things any better. By the end of the coaching programme, Charlotte spent more time in the sessions creating solutions to deal with the issues she faced rather than complain about them. As well as becoming aware of her limiting beliefs, she started to observe how they made her behave and used her skills to address them and take action.

THINGS for YOU to DO

IF YOU EXAMINE YOUR INNER DIALOGUE OR SELF TALK, THEN YOUR LIMITING BELIEFS WILL EMERGE

There are conversations that you have with yourself on a daily basis. Listening to them is essential, as they not only reveal what you believe about yourself and your work, but it is the first step in shifting negative beliefs and replacing them with positive ones.

To start making changes, ask yourself the following question: 'What limiting beliefs do I have about my career and working life?' Write down the first five that come into your mind. The act of doing this brings these beliefs out into the open, where they will seem less powerful and you can view them objectively.

Finally, in the first column of the table over the page, make a list of every single limiting belief that you have discovered. Beside each one, write down the thoughts, words and actions that it generates.

continued...

Limiting belief	Thoughts	Words	Actions
I'm afraid of conflict	I don't like confrontation	That's fine by me	Withdrawing from others
I'm not good at this	What if I get it wrong	I'd rather not have a go	Letting opportunity pass you by
I don't belong here	I need to get out	How can I leave?	Under-performing on the job

In the next table, you are going to build a list of empowering beliefs and actions to counteract the limiting ones. Put this list somewhere you can see it every day (either at work or at home), so you can keep these in mind.

Limiting belief	Empowering belief	Words	Actions
I'm afraid of conflict	I can take a stand	I would like to talk with you about...	Learn conflict handling techniques
I'm not good at this	I have the ability to try new things	I have done this a few times but it doesn't seem to work, can you help?	Taking opportunities and having another go
I don't belong here	I will make the most of this for now	I am going to make more of an effort to enjoy the work I do	Find a positive role model and ask them for help

continued...

Limiting beliefs can destroy your career, so whenever negative or fearful thoughts come up, acknowledge them. Then replace them with an empowering belief and follow this up with the appropriate words and actions.

MAINTAINING EMPOWERING BELIEFS

Once you have begun to shift negative beliefs and replace them with empowering ones, it is essential to keep going. You will find that the limiting beliefs won't have the same emotional energy that they once had, and in the long run, this will help to raise your self-confidence and give you a healthy and positive outlook on life. There are many ways of doing this:

- **Reading books and watching films that are inspiring**
- **Rewarding significant changes in your thinking and behaviour with a mini celebration such as buying flowers or going to the cinema or out for a meal**
- **Joining a professional network of people who share your values and are a source of support**
- **Asking for feedback about how you are doing from people you trust and respect**
- **Attending seminars and events with motivational speakers, particularly those who have overcome difficulties in their working life**
- **Keeping a career diary and reviewing it weekly or monthly to monitor and record the positive changes**

- **Running or spending time in nature to clear away mental cobwebs and get a fresh perspective on career dilemmas**
- **Taking an annual weekend retreat to reflect on your career over the past year to examine what has gone well, what hasn't gone well and what you want to do differently the following year. This time out will refocus and energise you to make the most of your career**

HOW I DEALT WITH MY LIMITING BELIEFS

Confronting your beliefs can feel like an uphill struggle, but it really is worth it. Prior to Millennium Eve I complained to anyone who would listen, that I no longer enjoyed my work. My limiting belief was 'I can't do anything about my situation' and my 'self talk' (I know I am not the only person who talks to themselves!) was 'I have to stay in my job and put up with how I'm feeling because I can't let my boss, the team and the business down. They need me.' This inner dialogue left me feeling like a victim and full of self-pity!

Such limiting beliefs were adversely affecting my attitude and hindering my enjoyment of working life. At times it seemed as if nasty little gremlins had been let loose inside my mind!

These beliefs meant that I worked hard and made the most of every opportunity. Whilst this might sound positive, these actions were fuelled by fear: I didn't want my line manager to know how much of a fraud I was feeling and covered up my true emotions by overworking.

For me, putting in the extra hours paid off. I was recognised as a 'very good employee', who produced excellent results and had great working relationships. However, I still faced difficulties, experienced conflict, lacked self-esteem and continued to undermine myself. So, what did I do?

I chose to test my limiting beliefs by resigning from my job to take an open-ended career break (my family and friends thought I was mad!) to see if there was life outside of my job (my limiting belief told me that there wasn't). At the time I had no dependants, lived at home with my father and had some savings. I had weighed up the pros and cons and felt I had nothing to lose.

Guess what? My limiting beliefs were unfounded and during an eight-month career break I spent time travelling, reading personal-development books, getting fit and making new friends. There was life outside of Marks and Spencer! A whole new world had opened up for me to explore and I loved it. I was free at last! Towards the end of my career break I was offered some freelance work, which I very much enjoyed and it stood me in good stead when I decided to become my own boss a few years later.

If you don't take action to minimise your limiting beliefs, then *The Career Itch* will grow in intensity. I am not suggesting that the drastic action of resigning is suitable for everyone, but it may be right for some (especially if you have been putting it off). In my case it shattered many of these limiting beliefs and created space for new empowering ones to take their place.

WHEN BELIEFS DON'T SHIFT...

Having limiting beliefs is part of being human, but you can consciously choose empowering ones and learn to respond to people and situations rather than reacting. If you do this often enough then you can even start to anticipate negative beliefs, evaluate them objectively, and have a strategy in place to handle them.

However, you may have emotional scars and deep-rooted issues that hinder the process of thinking differently. These may have more to do with your upbringing and personal life than your career, but they will affect what you say and do at work even if you are unaware of it.

For example, painful memories from the past may be triggered by people or situations at work, or you may have been left with a mass of limiting beliefs that won't disappear overnight. Whilst these can be overcome, it may take longer and require some additional help to restore your perceptions of what is going on around you and build your self-belief.

I have had a number of clients who struggled to shift their thinking because of personal (sometimes traumatic) circumstances from the past and in these cases referred them on for further assistance. If you think that this applies to you, there are counsellors who are better placed to support you in this longer-term emotional and mental healing process. You will find some details of whom to contact in the 'Must Have Resources' section at the back of this book.

WHAT DO YOU NEED?

"Patience is the companion of wisdom"

Saint Augustine

As a career coach I am regularly contacted by individuals who are ready to jump ship from the work that they do! *The Career Itch* has become so intolerable for them that they want an instant solution. I usually ask them three questions to stop them in their tracks and encourage them to consider their priorities. These are:

 Are you in a financially secure position to leave your job in the next one to three months?

 How much longer can you tolerate your current work situation?

What can you do to satisfy your work needs during the next six months?

What follows is an open conversation about their financial commitments from paying the mortgage to repaying debts, although I don't need to know the finer details. The money issue comes up a lot and I can hear the discomfort and resistance in a client's voice as I broach the subject. They would rather not talk or think about it!

Why is money management of such importance to your career? Consider the fact that many people stay in jobs that they dislike or have outgrown because they feel financially tied to what they do. Seven out of ten of my clients admit to not knowing what they spend their hard-earned money on from one month to another.

Occasionally, clients have told me that they are financially stable and have a sum of money set aside which will help to see them through a period of unemployment whilst they decide what they will do next in their working life.

Few of us have been trained in the art of money management and I certainly struggled with this when I became a freelancer, running up a large debt in the first few years of business. It took a while for me to clear the debt, but I did, and since then I have put systems in place to help me be more effective at managing money.

I had been so used to working for an employer, where large sums of money were available to fund projects, that I never really stopped to think about what I would do differently if the money was coming from my own pocket! If you want to become self-employed in future, you will have to learn how to handle your cash flow carefully, as it could make or break your business.

Often the emotional release that follows from talking to me about money matters puts clients in a more realistic frame of mind. We briefly discuss how they can become financially aware by monitoring their spending, living within their means, cutting back to pay off debts and then start saving. Alvin Hall's book, *Money for Life: Everyone's Guide to Financial Freedom*, is very effective at challenging readers to investigate their relationship to money and how it affects their professional and personal life.

If leaving your job immediately isn't a possibility because of your financial situation, then it is important to look at ways in which you can increase your satisfaction levels in your current work, while you save and plan your exit strategy.

Once you realise that there is light at the end of the tunnel, you will feel more comfortable about waiting for a while and making the most of the work that you already do. The moral of the story is that, when *The Career Itch* feels intolerable, you will always be torn between what you want to do, what is best for you to do and the timing of your actions.

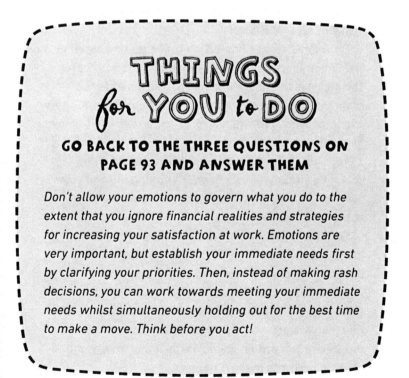

THINGS for YOU to DO

GO BACK TO THE THREE QUESTIONS ON PAGE 93 AND ANSWER THEM

Don't allow your emotions to govern what you do to the extent that you ignore financial realities and strategies for increasing your satisfaction at work. Emotions are very important, but establish your immediate needs first by clarifying your priorities. Then, instead of making rash decisions, you can work towards meeting your immediate needs whilst simultaneously holding out for the best time to make a move. Think before you act!

WHAT ARE YOUR ASPIRATIONS?

"Our aspirations are our possibilities"

Samuel Johnson

During a session on that weekend personal development programme I mentioned, I became acutely aware that I had no vision for my career, let alone understanding about what to do next. There was nothing to pull me forward, which helped explain the lethargy I felt. I left the weekend feeling excited but scared, because I had a blank canvas on which to create the career of my dreams based on my needs and aspirations. I believed this was possible. I was the artist!

Creating a compelling vision is like putting together a vivid mental image of what you hope for in your career. The vision is the destination point and a measure of progress or success. It encapsulates your targets, goals and intentions, and will energise and excite you to move forward in the work you do.

Your vision isn't fixed, but can be adapted to the changing circumstances of your working life and your own aspirations. It isn't supposed to be perfect, but authenticity is key.

On Millennium Eve, I could just about grasp that in one year things might be different in my career but anything beyond that was too far away for me to imagine. Your mind is naturally goal-orientated and a clear vision will help you focus. When you have a vision that inspires you, you will want to experience it and this desire will propel you towards it and give you the sticking power to make it happen.

ADE'S STORY

Contacting me was part of the solution that Ade had arrived at when starting to think about what to do next in her career. She was looking for help to gain the clarity, focus and direction that she desired. We discussed her career situation by talking about her work and looking at her CV and other supporting documents, such as client testimonials. All this built up a picture of her career history to date.

She had already done some work on her career values and transferable skills; this had become an annual ritual. Working as a consultant in the financial sector, she had a clear idea about her personality and talents, believing them to be a perfect match for the work that she did.

Ade liked the idea of creating a compelling vision that would help her map out the next five years and identify her future needs and aspirations. She chose to write a short story to describe her vision, partly to encourage her creativity as she was so used to being pragmatic in her day-to-day work.

I could hear how motivated she was and sure enough, having set a day aside to write it, she completed the final draft well before we had agreed to talk again. When Ade read the story out loud to me, I was moved and could see, from the huge smile on her face, that each word and sentence had captured the essence of her future hopes and desires.

Putting your compelling vision into words may not appeal to you. However, there are other ways to capture it. The important thing is to make it tangible in some way; this helps to bring it out of your mind and into the real world.

When I first read about the idea of turning my career dreams into a picture I was sceptical, but curious enough to do it anyway! I used the flower image depicting 'the job of your dreams' from best-selling job-hunting book *What Color is Your Parachute?: A Practical Manual for Job-hunters and Career-changers* by Richard Nelson Bolles. Years later I landed the role of head of learning and development at Costa Coffee and realised that this was my dream job (according to the flower diagram I had used)!

I have repeated this career visioning process every time I experience *The Career Itch*, and the results from it always exceed my expectations. This process is not magic; you are using the creative power or the right side of your brain that we all used in childhood (and which is always available to you). It is a way of clarifying your vision before you can turn it into reality.

ADE'S VISION COMES TRUE

Ade discussed the story with her family, and they each made a contribution to it so that it became a shared aspiration, rather than something that she would do on her own. Then they agreed that, on every New Year's Day, they would review their progress and add anything else that they wanted to achieve in the years ahead.

Her story was written in 2005 and by 2009 she had achieved two-thirds of it. This included developing her professional skills further by joining an online network and investigating the possibilities of doing a doctorate. She took on a new client who wanted her to create a UK-wide finance strategy.

In fact, having enjoyed the story-writing process so much, she shared this technique with her project team, who then used the same approach to create a compelling vision for the finance department. Ade's most prized achievement was buying a holiday home in Europe where she could take her family and then rent out the rest of the time.

WHAT ARE YOUR OPTIONS?

"If you do not change direction, you may end up where you are heading" Lao Tzu

ELLIOT'S STORY

Elliot and I met at a networking event. He told me that he had been thinking about changing jobs for over a year but hadn't yet plucked up the courage to get going. He admitted that there was no reason for him to stay in his current job because he had achieved everything that he had set out to. He identified strongly with The Career Itch because it summed up just how he was feeling. I asked him what he thought another job might offer and he vaguely mentioned things like flexibility and work-life balance.

Then, after what seemed like a long silence, he replied, 'That is a good question, I need to think about it.' We exchanged email addresses and I asked him to let me know how he was doing in a few months time. I sensed that Elliot's laid-back attitude betrayed the fact that he already knew what to do next, but something was stopping him from making the transition.

THINGS for YOU to DO

TO CREATE A COMPELLING VISION, THINK ABOUT AND ANSWER THESE QUESTIONS:

○ **What are the features of your ideal job?**
These could include the role, location, the industry, work colleagues, talents required, learning and development opportunities, work culture and environment, what the organisation does (products, services), and evidence of an active corporate social responsibility policy.

○ **Which of these three features would make the biggest positive difference to what you do next in your career?**

○ **What benefits will your ideal work give you?**
Here are some examples: challenge, recognition, security, salary, benefits, autonomy, variety and responsibility, work-life balance, a boss you respect, transferable skills, career development, intellectual stimulation, and making a difference to society.

○ **Which of these three benefits would make the biggest positive difference to what you do next in your career?**

○ **Add your top three features and benefits to your compelling vision**

continued...

- Is your vision congruent with the aspects of your identity from step one i.e. your personality, career values, talents and transferable skills? *If not, what can you do to address this?*

- How will your vision aid your self-development?

- Imagine that you can hear, see, feel, taste or smell your vision; what else can you add to it? *Engaging your senses makes it more tangible.*

- What resources, e.g. time, money, people, information, do you have available to get your vision started?

- How will you celebrate the progress and achievements of your compelling vision?

DECIDE WHICH ONE OF THE FOLLOWING WILL BEST EXPRESS A DAY IN YOUR IDEAL WORKING LIFE

- Making a collage of photographs, symbols, pictures and words

- Writing a short story

- Finding someone to record an interview with you (in video or audio format)

When your compelling vision is complete, share it with someone else. This can double your excitement around it and you can ask them to check-in with you and encourage you to keep making progress until it becomes a reality.

Now that you are ready to move forward, here are four options to consider as a possible next step:

 Stay in your current job and increase your satisfaction by taking on additional responsibilities, learning new skills or going on secondment

 Choose to change jobs and investigate what this might mean for you e.g. retraining

Go it alone and start up a new business

Keep your day job and start an enterprise you can do in the evenings and at weekends

Whatever you do next will be influenced by your personal circumstances and resources. Refrain from taking any action when you are at an emotional high or low, or you could be feeling restless within a few months as a result of not thinking deeply enough. How you feel is an important factor, but it is not the only one. Choosing the best option for you may seem mind-boggling, but you can do it if you think it through, address any limiting beliefs, and weigh up your needs, aspirations and options.

ELLIOT FINDS THE JOB

Just six weeks later Elliot contacted me to say that he had secured a new job at a higher salary, with greater flexibility and home-working, more holidays and other perks, such as a personal learning and development budget. Most of all he would be doing exactly the type of work that he wanted to do. He thanked me for asking him the question that had made him take action before his work had become stale.

I asked him what it was about my question that propelled him forward. He said that he had become complacent in his role, but our conversation reminded him of what was really important for the next stage of his career. Elliot had already done a lot of thinking about the direction of his career, which is why, I believe, things happened so quickly.

Perhaps, like Elliot, you already have some ideas about what to do next but for some reason or other you haven't got going yet. What might be stopping you?

WHERE ARE WE NOW?

Thinking enables you to get to the heart of what *The Career Itch* is bringing to your attention so that you can challenge your beliefs, clarify your needs, identify your aspirations and select your options. Ensuring that your working life is consistent with your identity and building an empowering belief system, will give you the motivation and confidence to choose what you do next.

Making a successful transition from where you are now to where you want to be is what step three is all about. Come with me!

"Opportunity is missed by most people because it is dressed in overalls and looks like work" Thomas Edison

is for

CHANGE

Making a successful transition

WHAT LIES AHEAD

> "We know what we are, but we know not what we may be" Shakespeare

Change will always feature in your career; you may be actively driving it or you may feel that it has been thrust upon you by circumstances beyond your control. When you experience *The Career Itch*, making a change of some kind is inevitable and essential. As I mentioned earlier on in the book, *The Career Itch* doesn't always signal seismic change; it is more likely to be incremental. Whilst this can feel frustrating, remember that it is not a quick fix, but it is about generating positive and long-lasting results.

As I've discussed, *The Career Itch* may come up several times during your working life. Managing change successfully is fundamental to bringing about a positive outcome in both the short and long-term. If you approach change with a positive frame of mind, consider all your options and are prepared to take a risk, then you'll stand a strong chance of meeting your needs and achieving your aspirations.

If the mere thought of change still feels overwhelming, then it may be helpful to recall The Serenity Prayer:

"God, grant me the serenity
to accept the things
I cannot change

Courage to change the
things I can and wisdom
to know the difference"

Reinhold Niebuhr, Theologian

CHANGE IS...

In all my years of coaching I have found that people struggle with change more than anything else. This has also been true in my own career journey. Making a change is about entering a new cycle or phase in your life. Understanding how you are likely to feel during this time is essential if you are to make the change successfully.

With this in mind I came up with *The Career Itch* change curve. This reflects the different stages that you will typically experience as you respond. It is important to become familiar with these as this will help you to understand your feelings as you go through the process, and reassure you that what you are feeling is normal. Furthermore, staying open to the process will increase your self-awareness and you'll be able to manage the various changes much more effectively.

I have noticed that many of my clients go back and forth between fear and demotivation, often spending weeks and months here. However, once they have a focus, this provides the impetus they need to move forward towards elation. You are likely to go through each of these stages, although how long you spend in each one will depend predominantly on how you handle change.

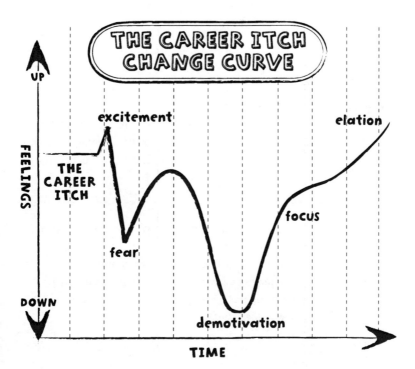

You may have feelings about change that are deeply rooted in past experiences (either good or bad). If you find yourself getting stuck in the early stages of the change process, it may be that fears from the past are holding you back or you may be anxious about doing something new. In the same way that you can replace

STAGES	Excitement	Fear
Feelings	Happy, enthusiastic, full of anticipation, positive, curious, energetic, buzzing	Vulnerable, confused, takes the comments of the negative comments of others to heart, anxious, stressed, overwhelmed
Thoughts	This is great. A solution at last. I am so thrilled. I know what to do next	I can't do this. It's all too much. Help! What if it all goes wrong? I'll do it tomorrow. I am scared
Behaviour	Impatient, taking action without thinking it through, motivated and starting to plan. Preoccupied by the new possibilities	Withdrawn, procrastinating, losing momentum, resisting change, inflexible, focuses on obstacles, sets unrealistic goals

limiting beliefs with empowering ones, you can choose
to treat each change as a new opportunity to move
forward in your career.

No one can predict how long it will take to complete
the journey from where you are now to where you
would like to go next, but you can get there in the end.

Demotivation	Focus	Elation
Fed up, demoralised, bleak, loses faith in vision and in oneself, uncertain, stuck, indecisive, hesitant	Hopeful, motivated, calm, decisive, reassured, centred, reinvigorated, realistic, confident, in control	Euphoria, expectant, apprehension about what is coming, sense of anticlimax, feeling of having arrived
I'm never going to fulfil my goals and potential. This is hard work. I give up. Forget it	I have reached the point of no return! I will keep going until I succeed. All things are possible	Change is great for my career. I hope this is the right move. Can't wait to start. I will succeed
Doing little to progress goals or stops taking action altogether, is easily distracted, depressed, lethargic, puts up barriers, sees problems not solutions	Reflecting, exploring, seeking information, gaining clarity about what to do next, comfortable with the change, calculated risk taking, making measurable progress	Building relationships, settling in to the new role, finding out how things work, setting up systems and processes, gathering information

ANSWER THE FOLLOWING QUESTIONS, NOTING DOWN YOUR THOUGHTS:

- What is your typical response to change?

- Where are you on *The Career Itch* change curve today?

- When faced with change, what stages do you tend to spend more time in?

Whether you are fearful of or committed to change, remember that you can always choose how to react to it. The Career Itch has brought you to a turning point, are you going to take it?

RESISTING THE CHANGE

> "You cannot step twice into the same river, for other waters are continually flowing in" Heraclitus

JAMIE'S STORY

Working as a project manager for a charity was Jamie's current role. He contacted me because he had outgrown this job and The Career Itch had already prompted him to think about what he wanted to do next in his career. He loved his job and felt that he was making a real difference but knew that whatever he wanted to do next would require some sort of change. Jamie was very clear that moving on was the right thing to do, but he felt anxious and overwhelmed about the next steps to take.

What Jamie faced is relevant to us all. He had become the obstacle to what he wanted to do next in his career. He was resisting what he saw as significant change and, quite simply, he was scared. Seeing *The Career Itch* change curve enabled Jamie to pinpoint where he was straight away; he was oscillating between the stages of excitement, fear and demotivation.

He felt relieved that his feelings were normal and realised that he didn't have to be trapped by them.

As we talked, Jamie became aware that much of his fear was based on feeling overwhelmed about what to do first in the search for a new role. He had been at his current job for eight years and had forgotten what to do or where to start when changing jobs. He also had a strong limiting belief that he 'should' know what to do first, but he genuinely lacked clarity.

Jamie was so busy berating himself for not taking action, that he was unable to direct that energy into job hunting. This added to his lack of motivation.

In sharing his career dilemma with me, he had lifted the mental load that he was carrying. Over the next few weeks, he did a 'back to basics' review of his career and shared his thinking with me. Jamie was encouraged by what lay ahead of him in terms of the 'focus' and 'elation' stages on *The Career Itch* change curve because this meant that the way he felt at present wouldn't be permanent. He understood that reaching the next two stages was very much based on his own commitment and efforts to move forward, and he started to gain clarity about what he would do next.

He decided that continuing to work as a project manager in the charity sector suited him well but that he wanted to operate at a more strategic level. This meant that he would be heading up a team of people. Although he had had some experience of this when managing project teams, he knew that it wasn't quite the same as being someone's boss. When I asked what led him to make this decision, he said he believed experience like that could add gravitas to his CV for future moves within the sector.

His career review revealed that before making the change permanent, it would be sensible to acquire some leadership skills, initially in a temporary capacity. This way he could find out whether working in this way would be preferable for his medium- to long-term career.

He had been made aware of a six-month secondment opportunity in another area of the charity and decided to apply for the role, which ticked all the boxes for what he wanted to do next. This would give him the opportunity to test drive a new role and gain some experience of being the line manager for a team.

JAMIE HANDLES THE CHANGE

His application for the role was successful. What surprised Jamie the most, was how much he learned about himself in the process, both personally and professionally. Completing the application form meant that he had to collate recent evidence to back up each of the competency areas that were being assessed. His CV, being so out of date was not much use, but he vowed to update it regularly from then on.

Jamie told me that even if he hadn't got the role, the recruitment process had prepared him really well for looking at another internal or external opportunity.

Three months into the secondment, Jamie was enjoying the role and had been nominated onto a coveted leadership programme being run by a well-known consultancy firm. The learning curve was steep but he loved the challenge, and he had been asked if he would like to take up the role on a permanent basis as he was doing so well.

His career review had highlighted the fact that he was good with people, which was confirmed by the team, and in a short time he had made significant improvements to team morale and the results they were producing.

He considered his options carefully and in the end he decided to accept, because he couldn't imagine going back to where he had been. Change had worked in his favour and he has never looked back.

One of the most important things that Jamie learned was to go with the flow of change rather than be intimidated by it. Due to *The Career Itch* he had got to grips with change and what he could and couldn't control. The secondment was enjoyable and opened up the path to becoming a director, which was the next goal on his career plan.

THINGS for YOU to DO

ANSWER THE FOLLOWING QUESTIONS, NOTING DOWN YOUR THOUGHTS:

○ **What can you learn from Jamie's story about how you handle change?**

○ **What isn't working about your approach?**

○ **What is working about your approach?**

○ **What do you think would help you to become more effective in how you handle change?**

The gap between where you are today and what you do next is not going to be comfortable. It is where you will test and discard previous ways of doing and thinking about things, and try out new methods. It may feel like unknown territory, but being in the gap offers opportunities for growth.

When I first experienced The Career Itch, *I resisted doing new things; it was some months before I took any action. My resistance was based primarily on a fear of losing control and my need for structure and continuity. On one hand, having these things in place made me feel safe. On the other hand, knowing that my career could be different gave me a sense that I was missing out on a new and exciting adventure, so when the opportunity came I stopped holding back.*

PREPARING FOR CHANGE

"Things do not change, we change"

Henry David Thoreau

LOIS'S STORY

We met at a fireworks party and began talking about what we did for a living. Lois was working in a human resources (HR) department as a personal assistant to the HR director. Her role was very high profile because she sometimes filled in when her boss was on leave (Lois had a background in senior HR management).

Having told Lois that I was a career coach, she started to look very interested, and her interest grew as I explained The Career Itch *concept to her. She was excited because she'd had a 'feeling' about moving on for a while but hadn't been able to name it and now she could! She explained that after four and a half years in her job she was restless and wanted to go it alone. Her idea was to start trading as an associate for a children's toy company, which specialised in making and selling toys for the pre-teen market.*

Lois knew that there would be the usual round of redundancies, because she was helping to prepare the communications, and believed that this time she might be a likely candidate. Personal assistants were seen as a luxury that could no longer be afforded in the challenging economic climate, so instead of reporting to one director she and her colleagues would have to report to three. Lois had already made up her mind that leaving with a reasonable redundancy pay out would enable her to start the business in eighteen months' time.

She decided to begin by trading in the evenings and at the weekend, starting with her family and friends and then expanding to local school fairs. As she loved the pre-teen products herself, she knew she wouldn't have any problems selling them. What Lois wasn't sure about was how to test run the business without making an absolute decision because there were other avenues open to her as well, such as offering her HR skills to small and medium-sized businesses on a freelance basis. She was holding out for change and wanted to prepare for it.

Being a self-starter, with excellent planning and organising skills, Lois already had some of the basic requirements for going it alone. What she didn't know was whether she could make a decent living from it. In discussions with me, she reviewed her finances and realised that there were some non-essential items that she could live without over the next eighteen months. This enabled her to save a small sum that would act as a financial cushion, rather than dipping into the redundancy fund that she hoped was coming her way.

She also decided to go on a six-month, business start-up course at her local adult education college in the evenings. The course was being run for free by her local borough to encourage female entrepreneurship. She mentioned to me several times that she was amazed at all the free stuff that was available to her and she capitalised on this at every opportunity.

Lois was focused and the start-up course gave her the information and insights that she needed to understand what it would really be like to run her own business full time. By the time she had completed the course, she had a growing nest egg and had sold a reasonable quantity of the pre-teen toys to family, friends and neighbours at local events, making a respectable profit.

Meanwhile, the company where she worked was, as she predicted, starting the redundancy consultation process. Lois pre-empted a conversation with her boss to say that she wanted to leave, if possible. She was glad that in just twelve months she had responded to *The Career Itch* and road-tested some ideas, before taking the final plunge.

LOIS SUCCEEDS

During one of our conversations, Lois had enquired about portfolio working and what that really meant. She decided to investigate further and spoke to several portfolio workers, whom she had met whilst networking, to find out more about the benefits and pitfalls of working in this way.

She came to the conclusion that portfolio working would suit her, due to her love of variety and meeting new people. Eighteen months later Lois was emptying her desk drawers and feeling excited about her future career. She had remained focused on her plan and was ready to reap the fruits of her patience, preparation and labour.

Today she has the best of both worlds and spends half her week as a freelance HR consultant and the other half selling pre-teen toys via the internet and at local events.

Lois was elated!

THINGS for YOU to DO

ANSWER THE FOLLOWING QUESTIONS, NOTING DOWN YOUR THOUGHTS:

- How can you learn to handle change differently having read Lois's story?

- What opportunity is change bringing you?

- What plans could you be making?

Lois didn't rush into making a career change but paced herself from the beginning to the end of the process. She realised that she was experiencing the complete Career Itch change curve because she stayed alert to how she was feeling and what she was thinking over the eighteen-month period. Doing this enabled her to behave proactively. She sought support and comfort from family, friends and her career coach when she found things difficult to bear, passing through each stage of change without getting stuck.

A GRACEFUL EXIT

On Millennium Eve, *The Career Itch* moved up a notch on the intensity scale and with this inner pressure building up inside me, I knew that I had to make a change to my working life rather than have the decision made for me. During my exit interview I was told that even if I changed my mind and stayed, I still had a bright future. When I re-confirmed my decision, the head of department kept 'the doors open' in case things didn't work out for me. But despite loving the Marks and Spencer brand and being grateful for all the experiences I'd had, I chose not to wait until the inevitable round of redundancies.

My decision was not made on a whim. I trusted my gut instinct that this was the right thing to do and the right time to do it. I had a small nest egg and my finances were in order. My self-confidence was high as I was leaving with some fantastic credentials and a great track record. I had done the thinking, weighed up the pros and cons and had a back-up plan (go back to Marks and Spencer!) if all else failed. I was leaving at the top of my game and ready to do something new.

So, against the well-meaning advice (and overwhelming anxiety) of family members, friends and colleagues who told me not to go because of all my achievements, I left. Though I had few supporters, I kept my focus on the possibilities that beckoned on the horizon.

There are times in your career when having done all the preparation, you simply need to leap. You may feel alone and as if no one understands you; perhaps they don't. Making the leap is an act of leadership;

you have to take your own lead! Remember that you are not the only person who has ever done it or will ever do it. In fact, when you have stepped over the edge you will find lots of other people freefalling, just like you!

A year after resigning from Marks and Spencer and taking a sabbatical, I didn't return. Instead I joined Whitbread earning 40% more in salary, with flexible working and a company car (I couldn't even drive, but had to learn fast!). The following year I was appointed as head of learning and development for Costa Coffee (my dream job come true), with accountability for starting a department virtually from scratch and managing a national team – my first! Thanks to *The Career Itch*, I had come up trumps!

PLANNING THE LEAP

> **"Many people spend more time planning their holiday than they do planning their career"** Grace Owen

Here is a reminder of the four options for what you can do next:

 Stay in your current job and increase your satisfaction by taking on additional responsibilities, learning new skills or going on secondment

 Choose to change jobs and investigate what this might mean for you e.g. retraining

 Go it alone and start up a new business

Keep your day job and start an enterprise you can do in the evenings and at weekends

As you plan and prepare to make the changes, there are some vital things for you to take into account in order to get the ball rolling. You will also find further details about how to do this in the 'Must-have Resources' section at the back of this book.

STAYING IN EMPLOYMENT

Your CV

I read recently that CVs are scanned in just 30 seconds! To make your CV stand out you may want to add one or two quality testimonials. It is also essential to ask for feedback about yours before you spend valuable time updating it. You can then tailor it so that it is appropriate for a particular role or job specification and conveys the key messages. You may even consider having two or more at any one time. You can get free advice on your CV at job fairs or you can consult a CV expert. There are also many specialist books on the subject.

Recruitment agencies

Signing up with recruitment agencies can sometimes feel like a hit-and-miss affair. Remember that they are representing you to a potential employer, so don't feel tempted to send your CV off to any and every agent, less is more. Recruitment is a relatively small world and you don't want to find yourself in a position where several agencies are putting your CV forward for the same job!

Do your research and be selective. Ideally it is best to approach reputable recruitment agencies based on word of mouth or a personal referral. You are developing a new relationship and if after some time you find yourself drawn to one particular consultant, focus more of your energy on building strong links with them and let the others know that you will no longer be in touch with them. I have a friend who has been with one recruitment agency for many years. She likes them, they like her and they consistently place her in great posts.

Stay focused

Whilst you are hunting for a new job, don't neglect the one that you already have! I sometimes find that once clients have had the eureka moment and discover what they want to do next, they start making errors at work, become disinterested or even spend their time cooking up ways to sabotage their boss! Not only can your past come back to haunt you, but it is not good practice. Remember that you are still being paid to do a job. This can be tough, particularly if you dislike what you do or are excited about moving into a completely different sector.

Remind yourself that many of your skills are transferable and there may be things for you to learn while you wait. It is also worth taking advantage of training, on the job or otherwise. If your performance determines the level of bonus you receive before you go, don't jeopardise this because every penny counts, and you might want to put that lump sum away for another rainy day in your career.

GOING IT ALONE

Be informed

When you start your own business, it is essential to have plenty of information about the process. Organisations, such as your local Business Link or business library, have a wide variety of resources (some of them are even free) and case studies of business owners sharing their stories about the steps they took. Don't reinvent the wheel, someone somewhere has gone down this path before you.

Some of the first things that you should do are inform your local tax office of your change in status and open a business bank account to keep your personal and business finances separate. Getting some quality business cards printed and having a simple website designed will give you credibility when meeting new people and potential clients.

Technical support

I remember my first day of being self-employed. I had a laptop, a mobile phone and a printer. Not long after going solo they stopped working for some reason, all within days of each other, and I was very distressed!

When you leave employment, you also leave behind the IT helpdesk and technical team who could sort out any problem at a moment's notice. Due to the increase in home workers there are many companies offering IT support and online data backup services. Once again, it is worth getting a recommendation from someone, if possible. Either way, do read the small print so you know when the support is available, how much it costs and how often you can access it.

It may be tempting to become adept at fixing equipment yourself, but unless you have a real talent or skill for this, it will become a distraction from your core business. Additionally, calling on technically-minded family members (one of my sisters is an IT wiz) may sound appealing, but not if you suddenly need help late at night or at 5am, when you are trying to meet a client deadline. Have a contingency plan in place should the equipment that you use falter!

Money matters

If you need to retrain, purchase a lease or buy equipment, think about where the money will come from, whether this is your savings, a bank loan, business angels or your family. Think about this well in advance, because not only do you need to run your business you also need to pay for services rendered to you.

When you work for yourself time really is money. Setting up systems to record your income and expenditure is fairly simple, although as time goes on you may find it useful to have an accountant rather than trying to manage the more complex financial aspects yourself.

I have found that, in the long term, hiring someone for a few days a year is a much better option than me taking a few weeks!

Purchase only what you need. It may be tempting to buy the latest mobile phone or upgrade your laptop, but think it through first. Ask yourself if a new piece of technology will really benefit the work that you do. It is important to safeguard your precious financial resources, which you may need to pay off your tax bill for example. Always be prudent because this approach will pay off.

THE BEST OF BOTH WORLDS

If you have decided that being employed and doing your own thing appeals to you, think about how this could work best for you. I have met people that work in this way because it is a good fit for their personality, career values, talents and skills. So, whether the day job feels mundane or you enjoy what you do, having another business interest can add a new dimension to your working life and bring in additional income. You may also find that you will have more empathy for your employer, as you learn what it is like being on the other side of the fence.

It is important to try this out over a reasonable period of time, such as six to nine months. By then the honeymoon effect will have worn off and you will be able to find out what it is really like juggling the day job, your business in the evening and life in general.

Having shared some specific hints and tips for three of the options, here are some general ones that are important regardless of the one you choose. If you adhere to these, then when *The Career Itch* nags you once more, you will already be set for long-term career success.

CAREER ESSENTIALS

Researching the market

Keep a close eye on what is happening outside your world of work and within it, by reading newspapers and industry magazines, listening to the radio and watching relevant television programmes. Subscribing to relevant internet Rich Site Summary (RSS) feeds can also be a useful source of information, not just in the UK, but globally. External changes are likely to have an effect, directly or indirectly, on the work that you do and the career path that you have chosen.

Political developments, economic cycles, social

trends, technological advances, changes in legislation and environmental concerns are some examples of external changes to keep an ear open for. What about internal ones? I have found that listening to the official line and unofficial line as an employee can present a more accurate picture of what is happening in an organisation. Be aware though, that the grapevine is not always as accurate as it is active.

As a freelancer, I speak to other specialists in their field at networking events and at conferences or seminars. Clients are always happy to share their perspective too. This gives me valuable insights into how change is affecting them and enables me to adapt my services and products accordingly.

Networking

Promoting your personal brand is now the norm and whilst keeping your CV up to date or designing a website to market your business is important, you also need to be out and about meeting new people and building relationships. Research has shown, time and time again, that your personal and professional networks are key for accessing new opportunities once you know what you want to do next.

Networking is not simply about attending an event or joining an online network, it is about mastering a new skill. Many people view it as selling, but true networking is about seeing how you can help someone else, either through sharing information, introducing them to someone or giving them a new business referral. This will develop your network and your generosity will come back to you, possibly from the person you helped, or more often from someone else.

The key is to minimise your investment of time and resources but to maximise the outcome and results of your effort. There are a variety of resources – books, DVDs and websites – that are great for helping you to think more strategically about the events you attend and about how to promote yourself with confidence.

Learning

Keeping your knowledge, skills and experience up to date is your responsibility. So whether you are offered a place on a coveted internal training course or you sign up for a personal development weekend, ensure it is relevant to your longer-term career aspirations.

If you are making the transition into a new sector and this requires that you retrain, it's worth asking for recommendations about the best training providers.

There is now a multitude of ways to learn, whether it is face to face, in groups, online, audio or visual. You can learn something new every day if you pay close attention to what is going on around you. Set yourself a small budget each year for self-development and spend it wisely. This can have huge benefits for your career.

Support in the curve

Hiring a career coach, finding a mentor or having a role model, getting together with a group of your peers, and spending time with your family and friends will give you the support you require. There are also great networks where like-minded people, who are 'making a change', come together and encourage each other along the way.

No matter how long the change takes, you will experience all stages of *The Career Itch* change curve. How long you stay in them will, in part, be determined by the quality, not quantity, of the support that you have. You are looking for others to encourage you to keep going when you want to give up, make you laugh when you want to cry and step back for a fresh perspective when you are too close to everything. If any of your 'support team' goad you, compete with you or are negative towards you, let them go. They will be more of a hindrance than a help.

Being accountable to people, who believe in you and what you are doing, will enable you to maintain a steady pace when you want to rush ahead and will ensure you take consistent action until you achieve your goals. Remember, to be supportive and patient with yourself as you make the transition.

Making an exit

Should you choose to leave employment, close down your business or take an extended career break, you'll need to put the appropriate systems, processes, people or resources in place to make the best possible impact on your departure.

Depart gracefully, don't burn any bridges and maintain your network of contacts because you may need them again (or they may need you). It will leave people with a positive impression of you and means that if you decide to re-enter the job market, doors are more likely to be open.

I have known people who have left an employer (resigned or been made redundant) only to return as a highly paid consultant months later. I have also known of freelancers who have lost client contracts due to budget cuts. Once the client started to miss the value they had been adding, they 'found' some money to rehire them. You never know when you may return.

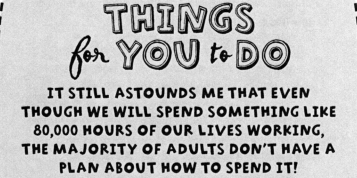

THINGS for YOU to DO

IT STILL ASTOUNDS ME THAT EVEN THOUGH WE WILL SPEND SOMETHING LIKE 80,000 HOURS OF OUR LIVES WORKING, THE MAJORITY OF ADULTS DON'T HAVE A PLAN ABOUT HOW TO SPEND IT!

Your career plan doesn't have to be long and overly complicated; it can be as simple as writing down the specific actions on one page of A4 paper that you are going to take next, over the coming days, weeks and months. Keep the plan in your self-development portfolio (see page 65), so you see it often and keep it up to date.

○ **List all the actions that you need to take, which will help to focus you on what actually has to be done**

continued...

Taking action over the next three months is a good timescale to begin with as it is relatively short. Then as you progress, extend the timescale to six, nine or twelve months, noting down what you aim to have achieved by the end of each one.

○ **Do make sure that the actions are written in specific terms**

You will need to drill down to the essence of each one and then prioritise them based on what you think or know has to be done first and last.

○ **Write down all the incremental activities necessary to complete each action, so that you can see exactly what is involved**

For example, reviewing your personal finances may mean talking to a personal financial advisor, collating bank statements, receipts, invoices and so on.

○ **Map out your actions to keep them on track and follow up as required**

You may prefer to start with the end in mind and work backwards from your goal to the present day, outlining things to do on a weekly and monthly basis.

○ **The challenge with making any change is remembering what you have committed to doing**

continued...

Put a note on a piece of paper, in your diary, in Outlook, on your mobile phone or whatever works for you. Allow yourself ample time to complete the action, particularly if you haven't done it before. If necessary, adjust your timescale instead of giving yourself a hard time!

○ **Revisit your to-do list to see where you are, adding anything new that has to be done**

If things aren't moving forward in the way that you had hoped, stop and think about why this might be the case.

At times like this I ask myself what is going well, what is not going well and how I can improve my progress. Writing down my responses helps me identify what is getting in the way and find solutions. If you decide to change direction this is OK just check that you haven't drifted back to the stages of 'fear' or 'demotivation' on The Career Itch *change curve.*

○ **Tick off each complete action from your to-do list and enjoy the moment!**

You can watch your progress as you move closer to your career aspirations. You may even want to factor in a celebration when you have completed all your tasks. I have done this in the past, and not only does it make you feel more committed and motivated, but it gives you a well-deserved reward to look forward to!

WILL BE BACK!

When *The Career Itch* returned again in May 2003 it reminded me that during my career break in the summer of 2000, I had made a note to start my own business as a freelance trainer, coach and consultant. This change not only suited my desire for autonomy and variety, but I had lifestyle aspirations that included marriage and children. Going freelance would give me the flexibility to work from home more frequently – and it has!

Get comfortable with the discomfort that change can bring. It has taken me years to do this, but I have learned (and am still learning) to enjoy the process of bringing about new opportunities. Responding to *The Career Itch* will take you out of your comfort zone, bringing fresh insights.

WHERE ARE WE NOW?

When making a transition from where you are now to where you want to be, nothing is predictable, particularly in the current marketplace; but when you proactively manage change, it gets easier. If you have already learned this, that is great! If you are still struggling, then keep going; and over time it will become more natural.

We are almost at the end of our journey together and it is time to move on. The fourth and final step addresses how to achieve a balanced lifestyle, whether you are still taking action or enjoying the result of your efforts.

> "Courage is resistance to fear, mastery of fear not absence of fear" Mark Twain

is for

HABIT

Achieving a balanced lifestyle

DEVELOPING PERSPECTIVE

"There is more to life than your job!"

Grace Owen

When *The Career Itch* gets your attention, it is a wake-up call urging you to increase your self-knowledge, clarify what you do next and make a successful transition to something more enjoyable.

The Career Itch also urges you to put your overall career into perspective so that you can achieve a balanced lifestyle, something that increasing numbers of people are looking for. The more balanced your life, the easier it is to make the changes to your career and be satisfied.

Although we 'know' that having a balanced lifestyle makes sense, my experience of coaching people towards meaningful and fulfilling work (employed, self-employed and both) has shown me that achieving this can be a struggle and there is no 'one-size-fits-all' solution.

I still remember the moment when a member of my team at Costa Coffee said to me, 'Grace, I really enjoy what we do and am proud about the progress we have made, but how can you help us all to achieve a more balanced lifestyle?' I didn't know what to say and mumbled something like, 'I will look into that' but, it stopped me in my tracks, causing me to step back and examine my personal and professional habits at that time.

My response was due to several things. Firstly, a balanced lifestyle was not something that I was familiar with. Having inherited an African work ethic from my father, the job I did became the focal point of my life and I assumed (wrongly) that this was the same for the rest of my team. Secondly, I did not know how to stop working so hard; I was on the roller coaster ride of my career, and wasn't sure when or if it would slow down. Thirdly, my career success was what defined me; if I did less of it, what else would there be for me to do?

As a team, we each explored and defined what a balanced lifestyle meant for us so that it would be easier to incorporate this into our way of working. I began by questioning my lifestyle needs and priorities at that stage of my career.

Prior to this role, I had worked my way up the corporate ladder, sacrificing much of my spare time to do this; a reflection of my work ethic.

After my first experience of *The Career Itch*, when I took control and gave myself an eight-month career break, I didn't have any major commitments like a home, husband or children. I therefore had time for myself to navigate the maze and figure out what to do next. Doing this took me in the direction of my dream job, working as head of learning and development at Costa Coffee.

I don't have any regrets about the different stages of my career and the lifestyle imbalances that I have experienced. Each one has led me on to something new and I have learned so many valuable lessons, without which I would not be where I am today. What I have noticed is that the quality of my entire life has increased every time.

When *The Career Itch* returned in 2003, I knew that soon I would be moving on to what I had planned to do next. This was to become a freelance portfolio worker, which I hoped would bring greater autonomy, opportunities to work in a variety of sectors, flexibility to work from home and the opportunity to be more than my job title.

GETTING INTO THE HABIT

Before I moved on, my team and I began to make adjustments to the way we worked so that we could each achieve our own balanced lifestyle ambitions. Although we each had a home office and at times spent up to 40% of our time there (the rest of the time we were out and about in the regions and at head office), it was necessary to redefine the boundaries between our work and other aspects of our lives. I had given 'permission' to make the changes we desired.

We planned in time for reflection, which enabled us to be more strategic about how we identified and addressed our stakeholders' needs. We had more social time together and created flexible work patterns. We had meetings around the UK rather than in one place to even out travel times across the team.

We pooled our knowledge and skills to spread the

workload, reducing the number of evenings we spent working late, so that we could spend time with loved ones, go to the gym or chill out in front of the TV! When I left the business we had improved our lifestyle balance, and could confidently say, 'there's more to life than coffee!' Achieving a balanced lifestyle requires you to put new habits in place; it's your choice!

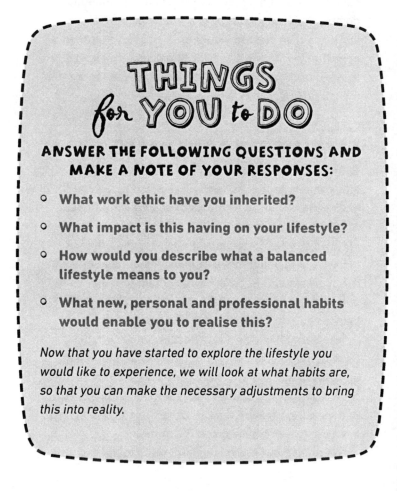

THINGS for YOU to DO

ANSWER THE FOLLOWING QUESTIONS AND MAKE A NOTE OF YOUR RESPONSES:

- What work ethic have you inherited?

- What impact is this having on your lifestyle?

- How would you describe what a balanced lifestyle means to you?

- What new, personal and professional habits would enable you to realise this?

Now that you have started to explore the lifestyle you would like to experience, we will look at what habits are, so that you can make the necessary adjustments to bring this into reality.

HOW HABITS ARE FORMED

Habits are established as mental patterns or, in scientific speak, neural pathways. Some research suggests it takes 28 days for a new habit to form but ultimately it depends on you. What might take someone else 20 days might take you 40 or 100 days. Your personality and extenuating circumstances will affect this. Throughout your career, you have developed behavioural routines around who you are, what you say and what you do. These habits are mainly subconscious and become automatic responses.

Being creatures of habit, we can't help developing repetitive routines because they give us a sense of belonging, structure, reassurance and familiarity. In extreme cases routines can become obsessive, turning into addictions. Recently, I had an opportunity to talk to a group of women leaders about lifestyle balance. I began my session by saying, 'I'm a workaholic, get me out of here!' because there were times in my career when I was addicted to the day job.

If you have never been great at timekeeping, now you know why. However, it doesn't mean that you will never improve! The problem we all face when changing our habits is that we give up too quickly, and so the new and desirable behaviour does, literally, not become embedded in our brains. Our impatience leads us to strive after instant results, but anything worth having takes time. In order to form a new habit, you need to keep doing 'the new thing' repeatedly, and gradually this activity will lay down alternative neural pathways.

Mastering your habitual responses is a challenge but something that you can cultivate. If you don't there are consequences, such as becoming overworked and burnt out. You may remain stuck in a rut or constantly hop around from one job to another without dealing with the underlying causes. The intensity of *The Career Itch* increases when you consistently repeat work habits that are detrimental to your life. Developing healthy habits to achieve a lifestyle balance will improve your wellbeing and your career prospects.

Forming new habits doesn't require you to be radical but it does require self-discipline.

If you find the word 'discipline' off-putting, then think of it in terms of managing and training yourself. Start slowly and make small changes to your routine that you feel will have the most positive impact on your lifestyle. It may feel tedious to begin with, but if you want to reap the long-term benefits, you need to be dedicated. If you keep doing it consistently, over time the new habit will be firmly in place.

It took me some years after that pivotal conversation with one of my team at Costa Coffee to achieve and maintain a balanced lifestyle. I love what I do, so I have a tendency to overwork (I know that I am not alone in this)! However, I have now reached a balance, which gives me a great quality of life.

It is not about reaching a state of perfection where everything in your life is equally balanced! I have tried to do this by allocating equal amounts of time to each area of my life, such as career, family, socialising, travel and so on. However, I was constantly frustrated, as I never managed this and my scales frequently tipped more towards one area of my life than others.

Now I know life has its own rhythm and I view my whole life in this way. So, for example, I accept rather than judge myself for putting in a few more hours here and there to get my work done. Similarly, if I spend more time doing other things, like taking four weeks' holiday at one time, that is fine too. I have learned to go with the flow and to make time for all of my life's priorities, which I have defined (in order) to mean:

- **Self care**
- **Time with family and friends**
- **Enjoying your career (already addressed with Steps one, two and three!)**
- **Being a volunteer**

CARING FOR YOURSELF

"Less is more" Robert Browning

PENNY'S STORY

This was our second career coaching session and Penny was telling me about her working week. She was up early most mornings at six o'clock, and went to bed late at midnight. This was the habit that she had developed over nine years in her job as a senior executive for a major public service provider. She didn't understand how she could be capable of leading a big department and managing sizeable budgets, but still be tired, irritable and look unkempt. Penny contacted me because she wanted to create more time to care for herself.

Penny stayed in the job because it gave her the chance to make a difference to all those who used the services and this was top of her career values. It was

*in tune with her personality, and she was well suited
to the role because it made full use of her talents and
transferable skills. Each time Penny felt* **The Career
Itch** *she took on additional responsibilities, and spent
a few days on visits to other departments. These
efforts paid off and she continued to enjoy her job
without making a significant career change.*

*However, despite her career satisfaction and
success, Penny felt as if she was running out of steam
and didn't know what to do next.*

In this situation the issues that Penny presented
seemed clear enough, but I wanted to know exactly
what was happening. To do this, I asked her to keep a
'time diary' every day over the next month, detailing her

CORE ACTIVITIES

Working	
Sleeping	
Relaxing	Cooking, watching TV, listening to radio, reading, hobbies, etc
Getting ready	Breakfast, washing and dressing, etc
Travelling	To and from work
Socialising	Family and friends
Chores	Washing, cleaning, shopping, ironing, banking, gardening, errands, etc
Self care	Getting hair done, pampering, having some quiet time, regular exercise, eating well, drinking water, general healthcare, etc
TOTAL	

activities and logging how much time they took. At first she groaned at the thought of taking this on; she was already up to her eyes doing other things and now I was giving her another task to complete.

When I emphasised that this would really help her see where her time was going, and then enable her to free up some time for herself, she reluctantly agreed. Penny bought a diary and got started. Over the following month, she had some initial blips when she forgot to write in her diary, but by the end of week three, she got into the habit of writing something each night before going to bed. She put all the information on a spreadsheet and this is a summary of what she showed me four weeks later:

| AVERAGE HOURS | | | TOTAL % TIME | |
Daily	Weekly	Monthly	Over a month	
10.0	50.0	200	35%	**Working**
6.0	42.0	168	30%	**Sleeping**
2.5	17.5	70	12%	**Relaxing**
1.5	10.5	42	7%	**Getting ready**
2.0	10.0	40	7%	**Travelling**
	5.0	20	4%	**Socialising**
0.5	3.5	20	4%	**Chores**
	1.0	6	1%	**Self care**
22.5	**139.5**	**566**	**100%**	**TOTAL**

What Penny saw horrified her and confirmed the concerns she had raised in the coaching session. During an average month, over a third of her time was spent at work. In fact, she was working more than she was sleeping, which explained her fatigue. Seeing that she spent such little time caring for herself meant that (surprise, surprise!) Penny's wellbeing and appearance had suffered. She simply was not taking good care of herself and it showed.

This stark wake-up call was what she needed to adjust her lifestyle habits, reorder her priorities and bring in some balance. Initially, she set herself three realistic goals to achieve over the following three months, which were to:

1 Go to bed at 11pm each night. This gave her an extra hour of sleep

2 Work an average of 45 hours per week by giving up some of the additional tasks she had taken on over the years

3 Increase her time for self-care from four to ten hours per month by using some of the time she acquired from working less. During this time she decided to have a two-hour massage, manicure or pedicure and take up jogging for thirty minutes twice a week. She also hired a cleaner to do some of her household chores, so that she could spend more time relaxing at the weekends

PENNY'S HABITS TRANSFORM HER LIFESTYLE

She continued to use the 'time diary' and at the end of the week she would review the hours spent on each activity and look ahead to the following week's agenda to see if she needed to make any adjustments. These habits enabled her to manage her time more effectively, giving her the lifestyle balance that she desired and protected the time she had set aside to care for herself.

Penny kept me up to date with her progress, and her commitment to taking action was inspiring. At the end of three months we met up and I was taken aback. Penny looked rested, energised, well groomed and happy!

She reported that she had more energy, because she was sleeping more, doing morning meditation and jogging twice a week; in fact, fitness was becoming a new passion and she was even contemplating doing the Great North Run. She was drinking more water, having suffered from dehydration, and she ate nutritious meals.

Penny's improved time-management meant that she was far more productive at work. Making the adjustments to her habits had been testing but had yielded tangible results.

THINGS for YOU to DO

ANSWER THE FOLLOWING QUESTIONS AND MAKE A NOTE OF YOUR RESPONSES:

- How are you spending your time each week?

- What are you juggling in your personal and professional life?

- Which activities would you like to do more or less of?

- How can you adjust the way you spend your time so that you care for yourself?

- What support might you need to make these changes?

- When are you going to start these new habits?

With the learning and insight she had gained, Penny had decided to take a flexible approach to her lifestyle balance, rather than aim for absolute equilibrium. Looking back over the nine years of her working life, she realised that there was a rhythm to the year just like the four seasons. In a typical year, winter and spring were spent reviewing, budgeting and planning, whereas in summer and autumn the public services were being used to the maximum and there wasn't much downtime.

Understanding that in any year there would be different demands on her time and energy, Penny already had her next goal in place, which was to take an annual wellbeing MOT and book all her holidays a year in advance. Penny was looking forward to the two weeks she had already booked at a spa in Greece!

Self care is not selfish or self-indulgent, it is essential. When you take care of yourself, you can take better care of others. Then you will be fit and healthy, perform more effectively at work and have energy to spend quality time with others too.

TIME WITH FAMILY AND FRIENDS

"Things that matter most must never be at the mercy of things that matter least" Goethe

GARETH'S STORY

I met Gareth having been assigned as his coach by his employer. His role was as a communications manager and although he was great at his job, he was feeling stressed. Most of the time Gareth loved the job but there were moments when the hectic environment and tight deadlines made him panic. This was increasing, so to stay on top of his in-tray and emails, he would spend most evenings and weekends working. He just about made time to exercise, which was his coping strategy and way of letting off steam.

As we talked, Gareth explained that he'd worked
part time in a bar following a career break. He enjoyed
this for a while, then experienced The Career Itch,
resigned and decided to take on a full-time job to
add a new level of challenge to the day job. This had
reduced the intensity but he was finding it difficult to
balance this change with the rest of his life, and it was
getting him down. Gareth wanted to spend time seeing
his partner, family and close friends (which had been
easier to do when he worked part time) but his spare
time was increasingly being taken up with work.

Having a balanced lifestyle is about understanding
what is important in life at any given moment; for
Gareth it was his immediate personal relationships.
Gareth's goal was to increase his level of satisfaction
about the time he spent with his partner, family and
close friends. With his priorities staring him in the face,
he wanted to gain clarity about where his time was
going. So he kept a 'time diary' over the next month.

GARETH PUTS RELATIONSHIPS FIRST

After a month was up, Gareth could see how his time
was being used over a typical week. He could also
see that there were so many demands on his time at
work that he flitted from one thing to the next without
knowing what should come first or last! He decided
that if he didn't get to grips with managing it, he would
never be able to spend the kind of quality time that he
wanted with his nearest and dearest.

He sat down with his partner to discuss the
outcome of his 'time diary' and to ask how she was

feeling about the lack of quality time they had together. To his surprise, she confessed that she was unhappy with it. They agreed that going out on a Friday night to see the latest film, or the latest art exhibition in the city, would be a good way to address this.

Next, Gareth gave his parents and siblings a call explaining he would like to see them more and apologised that work had been taking up so much of his time. They decided that having a regular family gathering would mean they'd be able to catch up on each others' news, without adding further pressure to already crowded diaries. So every two months they got together at their parents' home for Sunday lunch.

The next time Gareth met his friends for a drink at the bar where he had worked, he asked them about how they could all spend more time together. They told him not to worry and that they understood his job was a bit manic; however, they all agreed to make more of an effort, particularly for special occasions like birthdays, weddings and so on.

TIME WAITS FOR NO MAN

Having achieved the goal of spending quality time with his partner, family and friends, Gareth's next coaching goal was to address his time-management skills. I shared a simple plan that I had developed, with Gareth, focusing on key activities. In my experience it is easier to prioritise activities before breaking them down into smaller tasks to complete on a day-to-day basis.

Gareth made a list of all the activities that he did over a typical week (personally and professionally) and the events that he knew were coming up. He found this exercise very interesting because he tended to react rather than think in advance and see what his overall week looked like.

Gareth liked the idea of planning in chunks of time, because it gave him the flexibility to do different things over that period. This eased his guilt about having to account for every single minute of the day. The idea of having downtime also appealed to him because it was a flexible and spontaneous space that could move around in his week, depending on what was going on in his life. Having a schedule wasn't about setting his activities in stone, but about providing him with an

	Early morning 6am — 9am	Morning 9am - 12 noon
Monday	Get ready for work	Setting up the week, team meeting
Tuesday	Get ready for work	Communications work
Wednesday	Get ready for work	Communications work
Thursday	Get ready for work	Communications work
Friday	Get ready for work	Communications work
Saturday	Have a lie in	Downtime
Sunday	Have a lie in	Voluntary work

overview of his lifestyle at a glance.

As with any job there are times when you have to do things that you may not enjoy...for me this is administration! In the early days as a freelancer I tried every tactic to avoid it but found all that happened was that my in-tray grew! To deal with this I created something I call 'Tapas time', which is a three-hour slot one day a week when I choose to do anything I like, as long as it is on my to do list!

This habit gives me flexibility and freedom and I make it a fun time by putting on music or the radio as I complete each task. I love 'Tapas time' and the satisfaction of getting the administration done!

Lunch time 12 noon — 2pm	Afternoon 2pm — 6pm	Evening 6pm — 12 midnight
Meeting with line manager	Communications work	Gym, travel home, dinner, bed
Communications work	Communications work	Travel home, dinner, relaxing, bed
Communications work	Communications work	Gym, travel home, dinner, bed
Communications work	Communications work	Working late, travel home, snack, bed
Communications work	Communications work	Cinema, bed
Downtime	Gym, reading the papers, relaxing	Drinks in the bar, watch a live band, bed
Family time	Family time	Night in, dinner, relaxing, bed

GARETH MASTERS HIS HABITS

Having discovered that his employer offered an online time-management training course, he signed up to take it. Each session lasted just an hour and he completed it in six weeks, trying out a new technique after each session.

First, he started by getting into work an hour earlier than his colleagues, so that he had time to himself for planning the day ahead. This also improved his punctuality! Being technologically savvy, he used his personal digital assistant (PDA) to keep track of his work and personal activities. He also set up reminders for important tasks; otherwise he tended to forget them!

Then he created a to-do list from the many scraps of paper and sticky notes that he had amassed. He used a colour code, so that for each day of the week, he knew exactly what he wanted to achieve by the end of each day. Gareth had to be flexible, as news stories were breaking all the time. To ensure he was ready to react, he held one question constantly in his mind: 'Is this what I need to be doing right now?'

Gareth told his team about the new habits that he was putting in place (he noticed smiles on a few faces) and held a short team-building event to get everyone involved. Not only did this collaborative effort create more team spirit but it generated additional ideas to try out. From then on, every time a request came into the media centre, Gareth encouraged his team to ask whether it was urgent, important or a potential time waster. He also began to make himself unavailable for short periods and realised that the media centre would not grind to a halt without him.

Somehow, Gareth had exaggerated his own

importance which only added to his stress levels. Over time his team approached him less, becoming confident about making decisions and only contacting him in emergencies. Gareth noticed that as a result, he panicked less. He also became more able to say 'no' to unnecessary meetings; this freed up time to write reports, carry out research and edit stories.

De-cluttering his desk was next on the agenda. Having cleared it, he kept it that way by filing documents he was not working on at any one time. The filing system 'saved' Gareth on many occasions. He no longer rushed around trying to find information, because it was now easily accessible.

Gareth's next goal was learning how to manage his emails. Receiving over a hundred a day, he scanned them and only responded to those that were highlighted as a priority. His plans for dealing with this included answering his emails at designated times throughout the day and removing his details from group mailing lists. Gareth was becoming a master of his time and his habits, to the extent that his partner had complimented him on all the improvements too!

THINGS for YOU to DO

ANSWER THE FOLLOWING QUESTIONS AND MAKE A NOTE OF YOUR RESPONSES:

- Who do you want to spend some quality time with?

- What are the magic moments that you want to create with them?

- How can you improve your time management?

- What resources are available to help you achieve this?

- When are you going to start these new habits?

When our coaching sessions came to a close, Gareth was moving on to planning the next year, so I recommended that he use my version of an annual planner (*see opposite*). Visually it is much more interesting because it is circular, A3 in size, and can be rotated as each month arrives. It also includes the four seasons and the balanced lifestyle areas of self care, family and friends, career and volunteering. In this way he could make a note of key activities and events in each area for the year ahead such as downtime, holidays, visits, birthdays, anniversaries and so on. Gareth loved the idea and now uses the planner with his partner and family to map out each year ahead.

Gareth did not find it easy to put these new habits in place but he was motivated by wanting to decrease his work-related stress and counteract a frenetic lifestyle to spend quality time with others. By making a start, breaking down big jobs into smaller ones and doing the tasks you are avoiding, your time management will dramatically improve. When you are motivated by the lifestyle balance that you want to achieve, forming new habits won't seem so arduous. Gareth found a way to make space for the things that mattered most to him.

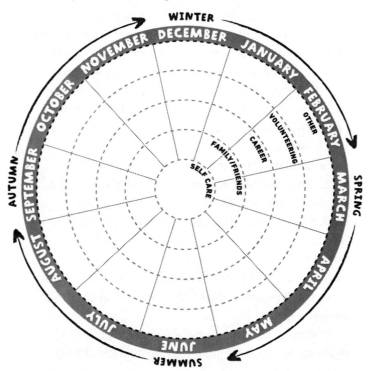

BEING A VOLUNTEER

> **"We are not here merely to earn a living... we are here to enrich the world and make it a finer place to live"** Woodrow Wilson

I had finished my talk on 'achieving a balanced lifestyle' to the diversity network and during the question time a confused looking member of the audience asked, 'how does being a volunteer help you achieve balance?' They went on to say, 'surely, being a wife, mother and business woman takes up a lot of your time and is enough to deal with'.

I am a volunteer because I love the buzz of serving other people. To me balance is not just about where and how you spend your time, it is also about what gives you a sense of balance through the things that you do. I like to offer my skills, knowledge and experience for free to people and organisations that need them. In return I gain friendships, insights and a fresh perspective on who I am and the world I live in.

I started volunteering as a teenager by working at jumble sales held in church halls with my friend's mother. This is probably what ignited my love for retail therapy and ultimately my career, as I revelled in watching people walk away with a bargain! Since that time, I have been investing in my local community in a variety of ways. We all have a responsibility, not just to be consumers, but to give back to others whenever and wherever we can.

At secondary school, I remember being one of many students who supported the Band Aid charity (and I have a picture of me with Bob Geldof to prove it!) because I was drawn to a movement of people who wanted to make the world a better place for those unable to do it for themselves. At university I started a creative arts charity with some friends, to provide a forum for people to express their talents though poetry, song, dance and music. This was also a vehicle for me to engage with talented people and be inspired by them.

Most recently I was responsible for the UK communications (writing newsletters and setting up a website) to promote a village regeneration project in Ghana, my cultural home. When I visited the village in 2008, I was moved to tears when the children, I had heard so much about, greeted the group of us who made the journey with beaming smiles. Taking a physical break from the UK reminded me of the contrasts that exist in the world and the truth that there is more to life than work – there is a whole life to be lived.

I chaired a management committee of people who came together to find a safe space for eleven to eighteen year-olds in my neighbourhood, in response to the knife crime fatalities that had taken place on the doorstep of my community. Today, I mentor emerging leaders who seek guidance and support to make successful career transitions.

DO SOMETHING THAT MATTERS

Most of us go about our daily lives caught up in our own habitual routines. Yet, there is so much going on behind the scenes in our local communities for you to get involved in. Doing this will add a different kind of balance to your lifestyle; the feeling of being connected to other human beings.

The most precious thing you have to offer as a volunteer is you! There are countless causes that desperately need who we are and what we do. You don't even have to travel abroad, just investigate your local community more closely. Find out what is going on by reading the local newspaper, visiting the library, the community website or contacting the volunteer centre.

What is in it for you? The opportunity to do something for someone else with no strings attached, other than to help them out. I have met the most amazing and selfless people through the voluntary work that I do. In reality you receive so much, such as developing a new set of skills that you can add to your CV. The experience of working in new settings with different types of people will help you to cope more effectively with different personalities at work.

If you are employed, most employers have a corporate social responsibility policy, so go and ask what they are doing to put it into action and get involved. I have met employees through the work I do who organise fundraising events, clean up local beaches, and wear a variety of strange-looking outfits for the London marathon. The organisation gains positive PR and motivated staff. You can increase your network by meeting new colleagues.

The possibilities for volunteering are endless. Whether you run jumble sales, help to feed the homeless, are saving the environment, lending a hand at the after-school club, befriending an elderly person or campaigning for human rights, there is something with your name on it. You can even share your career and working life lessons with others who have been made redundant or who are returning to the workplace.

Not everyone is suited to cooking in soup kitchens, so find a volunteering opportunity that fits your identity, skills, beliefs and availability. I don't think it matters if your involvement is ad hoc, regular or a once-in-a-lifetime event.

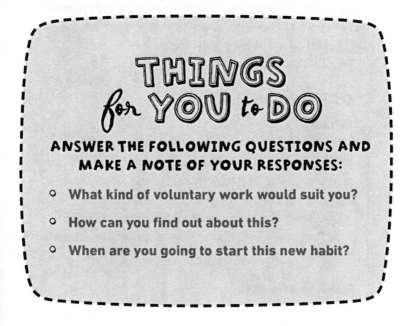

THINGS for YOU to DO

ANSWER THE FOLLOWING QUESTIONS AND MAKE A NOTE OF YOUR RESPONSES:

- What kind of voluntary work would suit you?

- How can you find out about this?

- When are you going to start this new habit?

HOW I MAINTAIN MY LIFESTYLE BALANCE

I have developed a habit of writing an e-diary for the past six years to maintain my lifestyle balance. At the end of each month I simply type up all the things that have taken place during that time in the areas of self care, time with family and friends, enjoying my career and being a volunteer. It doesn't take long, although it does take self-discipline to get started. I have come to enjoy the process, and not only do I have the space to stop and reflect, but I get to practise my writing skills too!

Here is a sample month...

OCTOBER 2009

Self care

Morning meditation – learning the importance of being still. It is a challenge as I try to quieten my mind and focus on relaxing. Attended the climate change day of prayer, thought-provoking and inspiring. Annual visit to GP – clean bill of health. Booked manicure and pedicure for next month, can't wait. Started another detective novel. Looking into whether or not to train for a half marathon next year.

Family and friends

Ben is talking incessantly and at every opportunity. I hear about all his friends at pre-school and in particular the latest toys! He is growing up so fast and his strong-willed character is blossoming, though discipline can be tiring. Simon and I went out for a meal at the local Thai restaurant; we love this quirky place. Planning the family day out at Chessington Zoo with our local friends; it is going to be so much fun.

Career

Attended the central London networking group for coaches. It was good to reconnect with some people I have not seen for a while. The leadership programme programme for the public sector client is coming on well, lots of great feedback about the improvement of skills to morale and engagement. Conference call for the women's celebration event next year went well and plans are in place. Away from home two nights this month. Received several emails about potential career coaching clients and speaking opportunities, the marketing is working!

Volunteering

Read the recent report on developments in Ghana, the school now has its own playground and pictures taken of the children on the 'twelve-seater merry go round' show them to be very happy. The school intake is up this year to 35 from 30 children. Simon is collecting jumble for the fundraising sale next week. Exciting to hear about my mentee's progress this month, she is starting to make headway with her business.

The e-diary helps me to keep track of how well my life is balanced each month. I can see at a glance if, for example, I'm spending too much time working. If so, I make some adjustments the following month by planning in time for myself, outings with my husband and son or visits to other family and friends. In fact, this year it helped me to make some conscious choices about how to make the time and space for writing this book!

At the beginning of the year I look back at all the

wonderful and difficult things that have happened in my life, which then become my means for setting goals for the following year. It never ceases to amaze me how much I get done in one year and how much capacity there is to achieve even more!

THINGS for YOU to DO

WHEN ARE YOU GOING TO START THE HABIT OF KEEPING YOUR OWN E-DIARY

?

STEP BACK

Time is not a renewable resource – once it has passed, it is gone. Don't take work too seriously, get overly competitive, or waste time by working too hard. Instead, create trust and collaborative ways of working; it releases creativity and is more fun. Whenever you can, surround yourself with people who boost your energy rather than drain you; but remember that none of us are perfect: we can all be 'hard work' at times!

Make the most of your time by doing the things that really count like caring for yourself, appreciating others and nurturing important relationships. Enjoy your career and share who you are with the world around you. Avoid burn out by refusing to work yourself into the ground and by not allowing yourself to be pulled in too many directions. Set aside at least one day a week to rest, relax and enjoy quality time with loved ones.

My favourite downtime is washing up (yes, really!) because that is the way that I stop, breathe deeply, become aware as to what is going on in my life and reflect on what is coming up next. A good friend of mine, Brian, once gave me some great advice when he noticed that I was struggling to achieve a balanced lifestyle. He said, 'Grace, give your energy away but remember to keep some for yourself.'

WHERE ARE WE NOW?

As you go about forming new habits that enable you to achieve your career aspirations and the balanced lifestyle you desire, enjoy it.

We have taken the last of the four steps together and our journey has very nearly come to an end. I have some final words to share with you before I go.

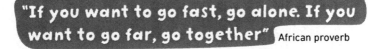

"If you want to go fast, go alone. If you want to go far, go together" African proverb

FINALLY...

"This is cause for a celebration!"

Grace Owen

WELL DONE!

What a journey it has been. I have certainly enjoyed every moment. This book has been my way of bringing you practical inspiration. I have shared some of the lessons I've learned during the peaks and troughs of my working life over the past ten years, to clearly demonstrate the amazing benefits that *The Career Itch* can bring you, if you are willing to accept it.

Your life cannot be put into separate compartments. Whatever you do in one area of your life affects the other, so in this book I have offered you a holistic approach with four steps for taking control: by knowing who you are, clarifying what you do next, making a successful transition and achieving a balanced lifestyle.

I wrote this book with you in mind. My intention was to support you, from start to finish, in forging a path towards the horizon and challenge you to own this quest. I know that it has been tough at times but it has been fun too. I trust that you have had the insights and breakthroughs that enable you to align your career and working life with what matters.

Completing this book is no small feat and your dedication will pay off with huge dividends. Now that you have learned to move from where you are to what you do next, there is an exciting future ahead that you can respond to. When *The Career Itch*, 'disturbs' you in future, you will be fully equipped to take control of what you do next.

WHERE ARE YOU GOING NOW?

Only time will tell. Whatever your career situation when starting this book, I trust that you can now see a range of possibilities up ahead. Over the weeks you have learned to rigorously analyse and audit your career, consider the big picture and the finer details. Be flexible with your options and learn from those who have walked the path, if you fear to tread it. Maximise every opportunity to enhance your working life, because taking control of your career is a continuous process of evaluation and discovery that starts and stops then starts again.

Having experienced *The Career Itch* many times I am excited to be on a path towards greater authenticity and integrity as a career coach, speaker and author. I have found and created a niche that fits who I am and who I am choosing to be. You can too. So, whether you stay in your role, change jobs, go it alone or enjoy the best of both worlds, the choice is yours.

"Carpe diem" Horace

WHAT'S YOUR STORY?

I would love to know who you are and how this book has equipped you to respond to *The Career Itch*. Visit **www.thecareeritch.com** and share your story with me and other Career Itch-ers around the world!

MUST-HAVE RESOURCES

This list of resources are just a few of the many that
I personally recommend.

I is for IDENTITY
Knowing who you are

Career Anchors (questionnaire and booklet), Edgar Schein,
Pfeiffer, 2006

The Learning Styles Questionnaire, Peter Honey,
Peter Honey Publications, 2006

Expert guidance for career development and changing careers
with over fifty years experience. **www.career-psychology.com**,
Siobhan Hamilton-Phillips

Walking Tall: Key Steps to Total Image Impact, Lesley Everett,
Lesley Everett, 2004

Now Discover Your Strengths, Marcus Buckingham,
Simon & Schuster Ltd, 2001

Myers Briggs Trait Indicator (MBTI) **www.opp.eu.com**

T is for THINKING
Clarifying what you do next

The British Association for Counselling and Psychotherapy
www.bacp.co.uk

Money for Life: Everyone's Guide To Financial Freedom, Alvin Hall,
Coronet, 2000

*What Color is Your Parachute?: A Practical Manual for Job-Hunters and
Career-Changers*, Richard Nelson Bolles, Ten Speed Press, 2008

*Minding Your Own Business: Survival Strategies for Starting Up On Your
Own*, Cherry Chappell, A & C Black Publishers Ltd, 2004

C is for CHANGE
Making a successful transition

*Who Moved My Cheese?: An Amazing Way to Deal with Change in Your
Work and in Your Life*, Dr Spencer Johnson, Vermilion, 1999

An online community of career changers **www.careershifters.com**

Business Link **www.businesslink.gov.uk**

The British Library, Business and IP Centre **www.bl.uk/bipc**, call 020
7412 7454 or email bipc@bl.uk

An online business social network **www.linkedin.com**

24 hour technical support **www.geeksquad.co.uk**

H is for HABIT
Achieving a balanced lifestyle

The UK's ONLY consumer event for health, beauty, fitness, healthy
eating and wellbeing **www.thevitalityshow.co.uk**

Voluntary Services Overseas **www.vso.org.uk**

Stress Management Society **www.stress.org.uk**

ABOUT THE AUTHOR

Grace Owen is a career coach, speaker and author. For over fifteen years she has equipped hundreds of leaders, managers and professionals to excel in their work. This has taken her into leading organisations such as London Business School, the BBC, Environment Agency, Brit Insurance, the NHS, Barclays Bank, Birmingham University, Camden Council, the Crown Prosecution Service, the Baptist Union, Marks and Spencer, Whitbread and Costa Coffee.

Grace has also equipped many people to make a successful transition from employment to going freelance or running their own business.

She has been featured in *The Times*, *Metro*, *Guardian Online*, *Red* magazine, *The Voice*, *Time Out* and *Pride* magazine. She was a guest speaker on BBC Radio Scotland and Colourful Radio, and in 2009 she was one of the UK's leading career specialists sharing her expertise with visitors at the One Life Live Career Clinic.

SOLUTIONS

COACHING
Individuals, organisations
- **A six-hour programme**
- **Face-to-face, telephone and email support**
- **Personalised for your needs**

SPEAKING
Exhibitions, conferences, events
- **Talks**
- **Seminars**
- **Workshops**

To make contact with Grace Owen or enquire about her coaching and speaking solutions visit **www.grace-owen.com**